MABEL

AuthorHouse™
1663 Liberty Drive
Bloomington, IN 47403
www.authorhouse.com
Phone: 1-800-839-8640

Book artist Rosi Gellenbeck
Photos by *Captured by Michelle*, Kelsey Gellenbeck
and LouCinda Zacharias Gellenbeck

Published by AuthorHouse 08/04/2016

ISBN: 978-1-4969-6175-4 (sc)
ISBN: 978-1-4969-6176-1 (e)

Library of Congress Control Number: 2014922908

Print information available on the last page.

This book is printed on acid-free paper.

All scripture quotations from the Holy Bible, King James (Authorized) Version, first published in 1611. Quotes are from the KJV Classic Reference Bible, Copyright © 1983 by The Zondervan Corporation; except Philippians 4:13 is quoted from The Holy Bible, New King James Version, copyright © 1982, 1983, 1985 by Thomas Nelson, Inc.

MABEL

A Demonstration of the Power of God's Word

A Hightower Book

Charlotte Huskey

authorHOUSE®

Thanks Mom

To Mabel the "greatest Mother" in the world,
I thank God for giving me a mother like you.

Because of your belief in me
And all the ways you cared,
Because of your support and
The encouragement you shared.

Because I knew you were proud of me
And the things I did,
Because I knew, without a doubt,
That I could count on you.

Because I had a family and a home
Where I belonged,
Because you were an example of
Faith that was really strong.

Because you loved with all your heart
And gave each day your best,
I know I had the greatest MOM
—- And I was truly blessed.

"I can do all things through Christ who strengthens me."

Philippians 4:13

Mabel May Kelley

This Book is Dedicated to the many Lonely, Hurting People in the World

Contents

Preface

"Come down here, Dink," Mama called. "I must discipline you for playing on the roof again. I have told you many times to not play on the roof."

I climbed off the roof into the cherry tree and slid down to the ground. I knew my fat mama could not catch me. I glanced back as I rounded the corner of the house. She stood in the doorway, hands on her hips, a determined look in her eyes.

"Okay, run if you wish. I will be counting." As I ran, I could hear the numbers mounting: "4, 5, 6. . ."

"Why did she always know what to do?" I questioned. "She is always one step ahead of me."

Memories as the above have prompted me to write about a woman who with a couple years of schooling had the knowledge of a child psychologist, the wisdom of Solomon, the patience of Job, and the love of Christ.

Mabel is about the early part of my mother's life while she was going through the school of suffering, learning to trust God's Word and His Wisdom. She graduated with highest honors.

May God bless this book to strengthen and encourage others that they too can pass through suffering and come out the better for it. It is my hope that readers and families will see the power of God's Word in Mabel's life and learn to use it in their lives to retain hope in adverse circumstances.

Questions for discussion at the end of each chapter make it useful as a family or class devotional book.

Mabel says good-bye to her only sister, Estella, when she is leaving Mangum, Oklahoma. Mabel is going to Oklahoma City to search for her papa whom she believes to be there.

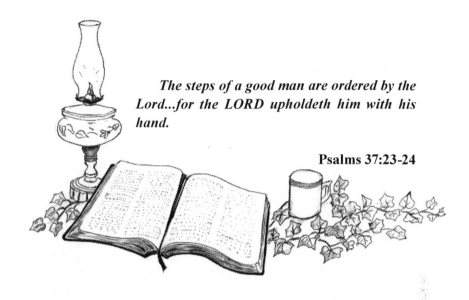

The steps of a good man are ordered by the Lord...for the LORD upholdeth him with his hand.

Psalms 37:23-24

SEARCHING FOR PAPA

I can do all things through Christ who strengthens me, Mabel said to herself as she stepped into the train bound for Oklahoma City. After paying for her ticket, she had tucked the few cents that remained of her savings into her secret pocket. In her hand, she held the most recent letter from her papa. Heavy fog shut out the spring sun as she waved good-bye to Wallace and Estella.

Mabel was 16 and had never traveled alone. She wanted Estella, her older sister, to come with her. However, Estella had no money; also, she was in love with Wallace and didn't want to leave him. Mabel had the feeling it might be the last time she would see Estella; she wondered if Estella was thinking the same thing. She drove away the dark thoughts by telling herself, *Estella will be happy with Wallace and I will be happy with Papa.* The thought of seeing Papa made her giggle. The woman sitting beside her in the train looked over in surprise. Mabel pretended not to notice; she did not want to talk. She wanted to dream, to dream of the happiness that lay ahead. She soon fell asleep and didn't awake until the train stopped at a town called Hobart.

Mabel looked out the train station window in Hobart, Oklahoma. She imagined the surprised look on Papa's face when he would see her. The excitement tingled through her, down to her littlest toe, and yet a gloom hung over her head. *What if she never saw Estella again; or what if she did not find Papa? Where would she stay? What would she eat?* Mabel pondered these thoughts as she waited for the next train that would take her toward Oklahoma City, from where Papa had mailed his last letter to her. She encouraged herself by repeating her favorite verse and the one she had read yesterday morning before leaving the hotel: *I can do all things through Christ who strengthens me; the steps of a good man are ordered by the Lord: ... for the LORD holds his hand.* Soon she was again asleep.

As the train entered Oklahoma City the following morning, Mabel began reading the street names. She was hunting for 12th Street, the return address on Papa's letter. She had never seen so many streets or such large buildings. These *must be real skyscrapers,* she thought. To Mabel, the four-story hospital in Mangum reached almost to the sky, but it would seem small beside these buildings. A large sign on top of a very tall building read, *Colcord. It surely must be a hotel,* she thought. Maybe I could get a job there. *Surely such a fine hotel would pay good wages and I could rent a little house for Papa and me.*

In the big station, Mabel watched people hurrying this way and that. *I think half the world must be here today. I wonder where each one is going and if anyone else might be looking for their papa they haven't seen in four years?* she mumbled to herself. She wanted to ask someone where to find 12th Street, but each one seemed so busy. Even the ticket agents were busy selling tickets and answering questions.

Before she had summoned courage to ask questions, she noticed an advertisement on the wall. It read, "Lee Huskins Hotel, Oklahoma City, 450 rooms, fire proof." Mabel caught her breath. *Four hundred and fifty rooms? They must need many girls to clean all those rooms.* After looking around a few minutes longer, she found a large city map on the south wall of the station and studied it. *There is the street where my papa lives!* she said to herself, her heart beating wildly. She stepped out of the station and looked around. There was the Lee Huskins Hotel towering over the other buildings. It was just one block from the train station. She wanted to remember so she could come back and get a job.

The street was full of cars, more cars than she had seen in her whole life. In the middle of the street going north and south were train tracks. People were getting off a little one car-train, while others were scurrying onto the little train. Overhead was a long wire that connected to what looked like an electric wire. *Is electricity pulling the train carrying all those people up the hill?* she wondered.

Mabel stuck her head in the door of the little train, "Does this train go to 12th Street?" she asked the driver.

"Yes, Madam," he answered. Mabel jumped on, pulled her heavy suitcase up the steps, and sat down behind the driver. "This isn't a train. It's an electric trolley," the driver told her. "Most people call them streetcars. Oklahoma City has 68 miles of these tracks. We can carry people to almost any part of the city. You new in town?"

"Yes, why do you ask?"

"New folks are arriving every day, a big hunk of 'um looking for work in the new Model A factory or the meat packing houses. There's been three huge companies open up meat packing businesses here in our city. Together they represent 3.5 million dollars, and some folks say that 2,400 folks have found new jobs with 'um. Why, the whole part of the city over there is called Packing Town because of those meat packing businesses." He threw his hand over his head and pointed southwest.

Mabel made a mental note, *Packing Town, is another place to find a job.* "This must be a very large city," Mabel remarked.

"Sure thing! It's the fastest growing city in Oklahoma, maybe in the whole big world. We're not very old. Just started in 1889 when the runs for land began. But you know in those few years we've grown to almost 100,000. Folks are boasting that we have 90,000 inhabitants now; and like I said, new folks are coming in every day."

Mabel gasped. *Ninety thousand people! Where would Papa be among so many? Will I be able to find Papa?* She trembled at the thought, and for a moment almost lost her hope. But she remembered God had promised to never leave nor forsake her, so she repeated to herself, *I can do all things through Christ who strengthens me.*

Mabel had never ridden an electric trolley. It went so fast that her head was in a whirl trying to see the buildings as they passed.

Before leaving the streetcar, she showed the driver her papa's address and asked which way to go. Following his directions; she was soon on the right street. Walking slowly along, she read the numbers on the few houses that had numbers. She was going the right direction. Soon she would find a number like the one on her papa's letter which she held tightly in her hand.

There it is, right in front of me! she gasped. Trembling with excitement, she knocked at the door. A woman opened it. "Does Simon Kelley live here?" Mabel asked.

3

"No, he doesn't," the woman answered. "He was living here, but he moved last week. He said something about getting a place so he could do his own cooking. I only rent out sleeping rooms."

Mabel trembled. She felt dizzy.

"You all right?" the woman asked.

"Yes," Mabel mumbled as she fought back tears.

"You look like you just seen a ghost!"

When Mabel recovered from the shock and could finally speak, she said slowly, "Do you know where he moved? I've come a long way to see him. He—he's my—my papa."

The woman saw Mabel needed help. "Say, Alfonzo," she yelled, "do you know where Mr. Kelley might be living?" Mabel heard a man speaking. When he stopped, the woman gave Mabel directions as to where she might find her papa.

As Mabel walked along on the streets the woman had pointed out, she quoted again the Bible verse, *I can do all things through Christ who strengthens me.* On and on she went, carrying her box that contained all her belongings. She was thankful for the handle, which Wallace had made when he tied it securely with new rope.

Finally, she found the house. "Does Simon Kelly live here?" she asked.

"Who did you say?" asked the lady at the door.

"Simon Pleasant Andrew Kelly?"

"No, he doesn't live here. Never did. Although he might be the man who came asking about an apartment last week. How did he look?"

"He is very big and has sandy-red, bushy hair," Mabel answered.

"I think that might have been him. But he never came back. There are more apartments at the end of this street. Maybe you'll find him there."

Mabel walked on in the direction the lady had said. She was tired and her box seemed to be growing heavier every step. She had left Mangum yesterday, but she had to wait for the next train in Hobart and changed trains again in Chickasha. It had been a long night and she had eaten very little today. She hurried past a restaurant because she might need her money later. The delicious aroma of food in the air made the lonely ache in her heart worse. *Oh, Papa, Papa,* she cried to herself. *Where are you? I've come such a long way.*

The manager of the apartments at the end of the street knew nothing about a big man named Simon Kelley.

Lord Jesus, please help me, Mabel prayed as she walked slowly away. *In an hour it will be dark, and I have no money for a hotel, and I don't know anyone in this big city. Please Lord, help me find a place to get in out of the darkness!*

The train station! I'll sit unnoticed on a bench through the night, she thought. Mabel was completely lost after going to all the different apartment houses. Now, where was the train depot? The electric train did not run on the street she was on, so asking first one stranger and another, she finally found her way back to the station. Dropping her heavy box beside her aching feet, she slumped onto a bench.

Mabel needed courage, so she untied her box and took out her Bible. Opening it to Psalms, she read, *"Like as a father pitieth his children so the Lord pitieth them that fear him...The mercy of the Lord is from everlasting to everlasting upon them that fear him, and his righteousness unto children's children."*

The next thing Mabel knew she was waking up. Looking around, she saw that the train station was quiet and empty. She noticed the ticket agent glancing at her and then at the clock. Finally, he called to her, "There are no more arrivals or departures tonight. The station will be closing in five minutes."

Mabel jumped to her feet and ran to his window, "I—I—I wasn't waiting for a train—" she hesitated.

"It's time to lock the station doors."

"I have no place to go, and no money," she protested.

"I'm sorry," he said, as if it meant nothing to him.

Mabel walked slowly back to the bench. Then dragging her box behind her, she went out into the dark night. An eerie feeling swept over her when she heard the door being bolted shut.

Mabel knew no one among the 90,000 people in Oklahoma City. Will she find her papa?

Questions for reflection:

1. Who was Mabel going to see?
2. How old was Mabel?
3. Did Mabel have faith God would help her?
4. To what city did Mabel go?
5. Where did Mabel go when she was ordered out of the station?
6. How did Bible verses help Mabel?

Mabel is locked out of the depot until morning. She has
no money and knows no one in Oklahoma City.

...In his favor is life: weeping may endure for a night, but joy cometh in the morning.

Psalms 30:5

MEET MABEL'S FAMILY

Simon Pleasant Andrew Kelley was finished teaching for the day. He locked the schoolhouse door in Pineville, Missouri, and said to Estella, "We must hurry home and see how Mabel did taking care of Little John and Mother Mary."

"Tomorrow is a special day," Estella said. "Mabel will be six years old. Can we make a pie or cake for her? Mabel loves sweets."

"I'm glad you remembered your little sister's birthday. I've so much on my mind lately that I forgot. Yes, she was born on the first day of October and that's tomorrow. However, unless Mother Mary is feeling better, there'll be no celebrating."

Estella shivered all the way down to the tip of her toes. Would Mother Mary ever get well? Mother Mary had been coughing for a long time and getting weaker every day.

When they got home, Papa asked, "Mabel, did you take good care of Mommy today?"

"Yes, and Little John, too," she answered.

"I be good boy," Little John said.

Estella went to check on Mother Mary. The bloodstains on her sheet showed that she had been coughing up blood again. Mary seemed to be asleep, so Estella spread a clean cloth over the blood spots and went to help prepare supper.

Papa was washing potatoes, so Estella sliced and put them in the big iron skillet to fry. Then Papa fried salt pork and made gravy in the drippings. Mabel took some biscuits from the tin breadbox and put them into a flat pan. Being careful not to burn her hands, as Mother had often cautioned her, she slid it inside the big hot oven.

"Fill the teakettle with water and let it be warming to have hot water to wash the dishes," Papa said, as he lifted the salt pork from the hot grease. Mabel filled the old, battered, blue teakettle with water from the large new bucket which stood on a log bench beside the washbasin. Mabel loved the shiny new bucket. It was not heavy or smelly like the old wooden bucket. She rubbed her hand over the smooth clean metal. Albert, her thirteen-year-old brother; liked the mossy old wooden bucket; but it was heavy, and Mabel thought it smelled musty and earthy. What she liked best about the new bucket was that it was not heavy. She could carry it all the way from the well, filled half-full of water. Papa placed the teakettle on the back of the stove to be ready for the dishes after supper was eaten.

While the food was cooking, Estella made corn meal mush for breakfast. Papa liked to slice the mush after it was cold, fry it, then pour a little honey over it. Mm mm, so good!

Clever Mother Mary had shown Estella an easy way to make mush. Other women sifted the corn meal slowly through their fingers, letting only a few grains at a time fall into the boiling water, which they stirred constantly. This took a long time and if not very careful, the mush would cook into hard dry balls. To make it that way was sheer torment in hot weather. Estella put cold water into a bowl and then added the corn meal, stirring it to moisten all the dry corn meal. This she poured slowly into the boiling water, stirring it rapidly for just a few minutes until it mixed into the water. In a few more minutes, the mush was cooked and ready to eat.

Mabel readied the table. She put on five tin plates and laid wooden spoons into each plate. She put tin cups for milk beside each plate. *One for Papa, one for Albert, one for Estella, one for my special brother, Little John, and one for me,* she said.

After they had eaten, Papa said, "Mary seems awfully weak; I think we had better slip off to bed quietly. Estella, get my Bible and read a portion to Mabel and Little John, then pray with them before going to sleep. We'll clean the kitchen in the morning."

"Come on," Estella said, after gulping down a few more bites of food. Taking Papa's Bible in one hand and grabbing Little John's hand by the other, she started climbing the ladder that led to the loft.

Papa had already left the table and was getting Mother Mary ready for the night. Mabel finished her food and followed Estella to the loft where they slept.

"Mabel," Estella said when they were all in the loft, "we must pray hard for Mother Mary. She is dreadfully sick." Estella fell on her knees and began sobbing.

"Why do you call her Mother Mary?" Mabel questioned. "She always tells me to call her Mama." Estella said nothing. "Why don't you answer me? And why are you crying so?"

Estella could not speak for a while. When she was able to speak, she snapped, "Why do you have to ask such questions, especially on a night like this?" She wiped tears from her eyes and looked away toward the ceiling for a while, and then added, "Oh, Mabel, it—it's such a horrible thing to not have a Mama. You see Mother Mary isn't my real Mama. When I—I—I— was very small, younger than you are, my mama got sick and—and she n—n—never got well. Then sometimes I had to stay alone while Papa and Albert were away. It's really frightening to be alone in a house in the woods."

"You stayed all by yourself 'cause you had no mommy at your house?" Mabel asked.

"Yes, and it was scary."

"Why didn't you go with Papa and Albert?"

"When the weather was warm I could go with Papa. In the winter the wind blew cold or the snow was too deep. Sometimes Papa had to go far away, too far even for Albert to walk; then Albert stayed with me and we played. Albert kept wood in the fire. Then the house was warm. One time he mixed sugar and cream with snow and made snow ice cream."

"I'd like some ice cream right now," Mabel said softly.

"I'll make you some on the second snow fall," Estella promised. "The first snow, they say, cleans the air, and the second snow fall is good for ice cream."

"What'd you do when it wasn't cold outside?"

"When the sun shone and the air was warm, I went with Papa to school. The big girls liked to play with me. When he planted the garden, I made pies and cakes from the freshly turned earth. It smelled so good. When he was cutting logs in the forest, I made playhouses among the trees using stumps for tables and sticks for my family. I always had a mommy in my playhouse. Oh, Mabel, I'm so glad we do have a mommy, and we have each other, too," Estella cuddled Mabel.

"Little John is already asleep, but let me read a Bible verse and we will pray as Papa told us." Estella opened Papa's big Bible and began reading, "*...weeping may endure for a night, but joy cometh in the morning.*" Psalms 30:5

Mabel interrupted her, "I think God is telling us that mama will be well in the morning."

"I hope you're right," said Estella, "for tomorrow is an important day. It's your birthday! Now go to sleep. Tomorrow when you awake, you will be six years old."

Questions for reflection:

1. How did Estella and Mabel show that they loved each other?
2. Did Mabel and Estella appreciate Mother Mary?
3. What did Papa tell them to do before going to sleep?
4. Why did Estella not want to answer Mabel's questions?
5. When Estella played house why did she always have a mother?

Estella and Mabel walking home together.

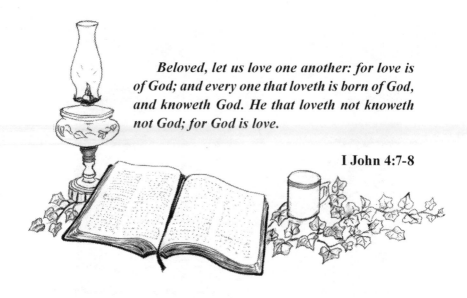

Beloved, let us love one another: for love is of God; and every one that loveth is born of God, and knoweth God. He that loveth not knoweth not God; for God is love.

I John 4:7-8

LOVE ONE ANOTHER

When Mabel awoke, Estella was already down stairs. Mabel could hear her working in the kitchen. Mabel remembered Papa had promised that she could go to school when she was six years old. She put on her best dress, ran a comb through her curly brown hair and descended the ladder, shouting, "I'm six now and ready to go to school!"

Estella looked up from the bacon she was frying. "Who said you were going to school today?" she questioned. "You have to start in the fall when other first-time students start."

"But I'm six."

"You'll still be six in August when school starts again, too."

"Yes, Mabel," Papa spoke up. "You are Mother Mary's helper now. You must help her and take care of Little John."

Mabel bowed her head and mumbled, "Oh, yes. But I really want to go to school."

Papa put his big hand under Mabel's chin and lifted her face toward his. Looking straight into her eyes, he said, "You will get to go to school. Papa always keeps his promise, if at all possible."

A few weeks passed and Mabel thought surely it must be August, so she asked, "May Little John go to school with me?"

"He is only two years old. He is too small to walk all the way to Pineville," Papa answered. "But I want Little John to go with me," Mabel protested. "Who will play with him while I am gone?"

"I know you really love Little John, but Estella will take good care of him and Mama when you go to school. Summer must come and go before you will go to school."

Mabel turned to Mary, "You still not well, Mommy?"

"Honey, sometimes I feel better and sometimes not so good. Sometimes I wonder if Jesus is going to take me home."

A lump came up in Mabel's throat. Tears filled her eyes. After Papa, Estella, and Albert were gone, Mabel helped Little John finish his mush. Then she put the dirty dishes in the dishpan and put water into it.

Just then, Mabel heard Mama coughing and she remembered Mama had said, "Sometimes I think Jesus is going to take me away." Mabel hurriedly ran outside so Mama wouldn't see her crying. She headed straight for the straw pile where she often went when she was troubled. Throwing herself upon it, she cried for a long time. She could hear Little John calling for her but she did not answer. Nearer and nearer the sound came, then she heard his little feet scuffing in the dirt. Soon he was tugging at her apron with which she had covered her face. "Why you cry? Want to see you face."

Mabel uncovered her face and said, "Estella says, '—it—it's—awful for a—mama to go away.' "

"Mama's sleeping. Mama no go way."

"Oh, Little John, what would I do without you?" she said hugging him, just as Estella often did her.

That night during family worship, Papa sang, "God's way is best I will not murmur, although the end I may not see." Then he read, *Beloved, let us love one another: for love is of God; and every one that loveth is born of God, and knoweth God. He that loveth not knoweth not God; for God is love.* I John 4:7-8

Mabel wanted to remember that promise. She hit her head with the heel of her hand. That was her way of telling her brain to remember.

The following morning when Mabel and Estella awoke, they saw that Papa had gone for Mrs. Tully. Mrs. Tully was the only one for miles around that knew how to help sick folks get well. Before she left, she said, "Mr. Kelley, Mary's a sick woman. She must stay in bed. You'll need to hire someone to nurse her and take care of the children."

13

"My wages don't stretch around buying food for a family and paying a maid, too," he answered. "Teachers don't earn as much money as other men who work only nine hours a day, although sometimes we work much longer."

"Mabel and I will do it, won't we, Mabel?" Estella said.

"Yes, me help," Mabel answered.

"We'll help Mother Mary. I'll stay home from school and take care of her," Estella offered.

"What a good girl! Then I'll help you with your lessons in the evenings. It's late now so pack a lunch for Albert and me. Put six biscuits and salt pork in the blue lard bucket. I will draw up plenty of water so you won't have to do that," Papa said.

Mabel followed Papa to the well. She hoped he would say she could go along with him at least a few days, now that Estella had promised to stay home. She watched the water splashing as he emptied the long narrow well bucket into the large round galvanized tub. One, two, three, four buckets he emptied into the tub. The well bucket was a light-weight pipe with a flap at the bottom that opened with the force of the water coming up into the pipe-bucket. It fell back in place when the bucket was being drawn upward. The continuous squeaking of the pulley lifting the bucket calmed Mabel's anxious heart. She liked helping Mama. Nevertheless, she so wanted to go to school.

Next, Papa took his pocketknife from the bib of his overalls and a bar of soap from a pocket on his hip. He began shaving the bar of homemade lye soap, letting the shavings fall into the water. When he was finished, she followed him to the house. He brought out Mother Mary's soiled sheets, Albert's dirty shirt, some print dresses, socks, and under clothes and put them to soaking in the soapy water.

Albert carried in the wood he had been splitting and stacked it near the stove. "Be sure to keep wood in the fire," Papa told Estella. "Sick folks have to be kept warm."

From the doorway, Mabel watched as Albert and Papa walked away. Tears trickled down her cheeks. Only her duty of helping Mama to get well and caring for Little John kept her from running after them.

When they had disappeared out of sight, she turned to help with the housework and nursing. "Now what am I supposed to do?" she asked.

"Put beans to cook," Estella said. Estella took the big white enamel pot, filled it half full of water, and set it on the big stove to heat. Mabel poured the brown dry beans on the table and patted them flat. Then she picked out the rocks and sticks. She washed the beans and poured them into the big white kettle. While they were cooking, she helped Estella wash the dishes; although she hated washing dishes. When Estella went out to wash the clothes, Mabel sat quietly near the bed so she could watch Mama.

Mabel soon grew tired of watching Mama, so she slipped out of the room and into the yard to play with Little John. First, they played on the rope that Papa had hung from the tree limb. Then they raked up a pile of leaves and twigs and pretended they were cooking.

When Estella put Little John down for a nap, Mabel went looking for something else to do. That is when she saw the clothes that Estella had not finished washing. They were soaking in the tub. The clean sheets that Estella had washed and hung out to dry were flapping in the wind. "I'll wash these smaller clothes and show Papa that I love him," she said. Quickly she found a low stool and climbing up on the stool, began rubbing her stockings up and down on the board. Holding up the stockings, she said, "Look, all the dirt is gone. I really can wash clothes." Next, she scrubbed Papa's and Albert's socks and her petticoat.

Just as she was finishing her petticoat, she heard Papa and Albert returning from school. Embarrassed that Albert would see her petticoat, she quickly leaned across the tub to tuck the petticoat into the new bucket where she had been putting the clean clothes. This caused the tub to tip. "Watch out!" Papa shouted, running to catch her. It was too late. The big tub had fallen, knocking Mabel to the ground and burying her in wet clothes.

"Mabel looks like a new-born chick just coming out of its shell," Albert said laughingly. Mother Mary's print dress hung over her shoulder, Albert's shirt across her tummy.

"Trying to help?" questioned Papa.

"I wanted to show you that I love you," she said as she trembled in the cool wind.

"I know you love me, but now I'll have to draw more water; and these clothes are not just dirty, they're muddy. You should—" Then he noticed how discouraged Mabel looked. He twisted his big hands together as he always did when he got nervous. "I'm sorry," he said. "Thanks, Honey, for trying— Tomorrow I'll put the tub inside on a low bench and you may wash again."

"Okay!" Mabel mumbled, as she ran shivering into the house.

The next day she washed the small clothes and hung them on a low clothesline that Papa had made especially for her.

Questions for reflection:

1. Name some ways Mabel showed her love.
2. In what ways did Estella show her love?
3. What did Albert do that showed his love?
4. Do you think this family loved each other?
5. What is the verse for this story?

"Oh, Little John, what would I do without you?" she
said hugging him, just as Estella often did her.

Mabel washed clothes to show that she loved her papa.

Thou wilt keep him in perfect peace whose mind is stayed on thee....

Isaiah 26:3

PEACE IN TIME OF TROUBLE

November passed, then December, and the long winter came bringing snow, ice and cold wind. Mabel and Little John played inside. When the weather was very, very cold, Papa and Albert stayed home. Mabel loved those days when the family was together. Papa made popcorn and they played *hide the thimble* and *pussy wants a corner*. Big Papa would crawl on his knees across the rough plank floor and meow like a kitten in front of Mabel. If she laughed, she had to give him her seat. If she did not laugh, he had to crawl to another person and meow for a seat.

Sometimes they sang on those days. Papa's tenor voice pushed all fear and anxiety outside into the howling storm, leaving Mabel with bright hopes as if it were the night before Christmas.

As the months passed, Mabel caught herself thinking often about how frightened Estella acted the evening of her sixth birthday. Sometimes during the night when Mama's loud coughing awoke her, she could hear Estella crying. Mabel would cry, too. Then Estella would hug her and repeat the verse, *Weeping may endure for a night, but joy cometh in the morning.*

One cold evening while they were eating supper, Albert said to Papa, "Didn't you go into Oklahoma for one of the runs to get free land?"

"Yes, I did. I was 28 years old. Everyone for miles around was eager to go get free land in Indian Territory."

"Indian Territory? I thought it was Oklahoma," questioned Albert.

"The year I went it was Indian Territory. Later Indian Territory joined with Oklahoma Territory to become the state of Oklahoma."

"Sorry I interrupted. Go ahead, tell us about it."

My new bride, your mother, and I were young and thought we could conquer the world. We loaded up our few belongings and headed for the Kansas border. Along the way, we passed by families waiting while getting their broken down wagons repaired. Others having faster horses and better wagons ran ahead of us. Some were on horseback. Many were walking. Hundreds of men, women, and children headed to claim free land. They were not all farmers either. There were doctors, pharmacists, lawyers, public officials, and men of all trades, each one going to make a better life for their families and themselves.

We were told that on April 22 at dawn when we heard the gun shot, we could cross the line and claim whatever size land we could stake out. I was new to the territory and didn't realize that many men had gone in ahead of time, looked over the lay of the land, and had their pieces already spotted. Some men also had their portions of land marked out. The men who went in before the proper day were called "Sooners."

Fights soon broke out over land boundaries. Many men lost their lives. However, many families were successful in getting and keeping their land. Those who stayed and farmed the land for five years could get a deed in their name from the government. Then the land was theirs to be passed on to their children. Some of the braver widows were able to farm their land and kept their claims. Other widows went back to their people so their families could help them raise their fatherless children.

It was a blessing to many who prospered, but it was also a sad time for those who lost their lives or those whose land turned out to be poor or without water.

"Did you get some land?" Estella asked.

"Yes, my claim of land was around what was later called Drumright and Cushing."

"Why did we leave it?" Albert asked.

Papa raised his head toward the ceiling and his blue eyes seemed focused on something far away. He wrung his big hands together and cleared his throat several times before he spoke. "We stayed a long time, my new bride and I. Albert, you were born there and you, too, Estella." Papa paused hung his head and wrung his hands again. "And then things turned bad. Your mother never regained her strength after Estella's birth. She struggled for several years." He raised his head and Mabel saw again that faraway look in his steel blue eyes. "My first bride is over there. It makes Heaven seem sweet."

"Oh, Papa could we move back to Oklahoma?" Estella asked.

"Well, I brought you two children here so my family could help me raise you. Maybe someday we can move back to Oklahoma. Right now I hear there are great opportunities on the Strawberry River in Arkansas."

"Will I get to go to school when we move?" Mabel asked.

"We aren't moving right now. Maybe when Mother Mary and Little John are feeling stronger and I have located a school that needs a teacher."

When spring came, the warm sunshine beat away at the ice and snow until it ran away in trickles of water down the hills, filling the creeks. Soon little Sugar Creek behind the cabin was deep again. Sometimes Papa carried Mama outside where she watched Mabel and Little John wade in the water or swing on the rope that hung from the tree.

On warm days, neighbors or relatives came to visit. Sometimes Mama laughed and talked with them.

"I think Mama's getting well," Mabel whispered to Estella.

"I hope so, but didn't you hear what she said to Aunt Martha yesterday?"

"No."

"She said, 'This will probably be the last time I see you.' "

Mabel stood horror-stricken for a moment and then asked, "Where do mamas go that don't get well? Can we go, too?"

"Don't ask such foolish questions," Estella demanded. "Let's learn this verse that Papa said to memorize." Mabel slumped down on the floor. "Repeat this after me," Estella said. "Yea, though I walk through the valley of the shadow of death…"

"Yea, though I walk through the valley of the shadow of death…" Mabel repeated.

"…I will fear no evil: for thou art with me; thy rod and thy staff they comfort me," said Estella.

"What does that mean?" questioned Mabel.

"That means we are not to be afraid, because God's Word, which is His rod and staff, will comfort us in any kind of sorrow. Even—even—" Estella couldn't say it. "Just learn the verse like Papa said," she demanded.

Mabel repeated, "Yea, though I walk through the valley of the shadow of death, I will fear no evil: for thou art with me; thy rod and thy staff they comfort me."

During worship that evening, Estella asked, "How can a person have peace when there are so many disappointments?"

"Peace has many meanings," said Papa. "It means people work and play together without fighting, like you children do." Little John and Mabel giggled. Estella looked at Mabel and raised her eyebrows. Henry Albert just grunted.

"It is also a feeling within us," Papa continued. "With God's peace in our hearts, we can be content when things make us unhappy. If we keep thinking about the good things that God does for us each day, we will have God's peace in our heart."

"I know a verse like that," said Mabel. *"Great peace have they that love thy law, and—and—and."*

"And nothing shall offend them" Papa said, helping Mabel to finish the verse. "To keep from being offended, a person must trust God's wisdom and not get angry with Him for what happens to them. If we love God more than any other thing, no matter how much trouble we have, we will have peace and…"

"But why did Mother die and Mother Mary get so sick?" Estella moaned.

"God knows what is best," answered Papa. "Perhaps He knows we will try harder to live right if we have someone in Heaven to go see."

21

Questions for reflection:

1. Why did Mabel like cold icy weather?
2. What effect did Papa's singing have?
3. Was being with family important to Mabel?
4. Why did Papa leave Oklahoma?
5. Do you think Papa loved his family more than land or riches?
6. What should we do to keep peace in our heart?

This is Mabel's grand children and friends reenacting
the Oklahoma Land Run of 1889.

Albert playing with Little John.

Yea, though I walk through the valley of the shadow of death, I will fear no evil: for thou art with me; thy rod and thy staff they comfort me.

Psalms 23:4

MOVING TO NEOSHO

Mama's sickness was a cloud that hung always over the Kelley family. It weighed on their heads and on their shoulders. It was like running a race against someone much older and larger than yourself. Sometimes it made them feel weak and made breathing difficult.

One evening Papa called the children outside. "News came today that Grandpa Williams is very ill. I've already been thinking that since the weather has cooled off we should move near them. We can probably find work on Grandma Crumbliss' farm, not far from Neosho. I'm sure Mary would like to be near her family. Perhaps it would help her recover. So let's get our clothes washed today and tomorrow we will cook enough food to last two days. Then we can go."

Albert drew many buckets of water from the well. Estella and Mabel washed all day. The clothes line and all the bushes around their log cabin were covered with clean clothes they had hung there to dry. They also kept a pot of beans cooking over a little fire outside. The following morning Mabel and Little John ran in and out of the tall grass and bushes, hunting hens' nests that might have eggs. Papa helped Estella bake bread. They boiled potatoes and the eggs they found. Papa pulled the old straw out of the mattress covers and put new straw into two of them. Estella washed the others; and after they were dry, she folded and packed them in the wagon. All day long they worked. That night they slept on the floor without the straw-filled mattresses. Only Mother Mary slept on the two newly-filled straw mattresses.

When everything was ready for the move, Papa carried out the two straw mattresses and placed them in the wagon for Mary to lie on. Estella tied their clean clothes in bundles and put them beside Mary as pillows to cushion the bumps and jolts of the wagon. Albert carried out the big washtub full of dishes, pots and pans. Mabel filled the shiny new bucket with cracked corn for the chickens. Last of all, Papa tied on the chicken coop with the hens and the old rooster. "As long as we have hens, we'll have eggs," he said. "Eggs are what Mary needs to get well."

They started early in the morning. Often through the day they stopped to let Mama rest. Just before dark, they arrived at Grandpa Williams' home southeast of Neosho.

Neosho was a much larger city than either Pineville or Goodman. In the 1900 census, Neosho's population was 2,725 persons. Although there had been no major battles of the Civil war fought there, much of the city had been burned. The newly reconstructed city had many red brick structures built around the courthouse. The four story Hass Building on the north side of the square is one of those. Neosho had a lumberyard, livery stables, general stores, a mill, and several manufacturing companies, including a wagon manufacturer. The Kansas City-Fort Smith and Southern Railroad lines served the city. The Missouri and North Arkansas Railroad came from Eureka Springs to Neosho. The Neosho National Fish Hatchery was in operation. Fish raised here were released to live in the wild in the many rivers, creeks and lakes in the surrounding area. Because of the nine fresh water springs in the area, it is called Neosho. The word "Neosho" in some Native American languages means "clear or abundant water." Big Spring Park was a popular attraction as well as Monark Springs three miles east of Neosho.

A few years before Mabel's family moved into the area, Monark Springs came to international attention. Hermann Jaeger, a Swiss immigrant, and his brother, John, developed a very strong grape plant by crossing an eastern domestic grape and a Missouri wild grape. At that time in France, Spain, and Portugal, the phylloxera louse was destroying vineyards. Jaeger sent cuttings of his grape plants to Europe. The louse did not destroy his grape plants. Many people around Neosho found work in Hermann's vineyards, cultivating and shipping hundreds and hundreds of cuttings to Europe. Hermann Jaeger became a rich man. He also received the France Legion of Honor. That is the highest honor that France gives to a civilian. In 1895, Hermann Jaeger disappeared; no one knew what happened to him.

Neosho area also had many schools. Papa read about them in the local weekly newspaper. However, Mother Mary needed Papa to help her adjust to the changes. A month passed and another month. Mabel was getting her hopes up that the move was helping Mama and that Mama would soon be well enough so that Mabel could go to school. Then dreadful news came that Grandpa Williams had died. When Papa went in to tell Mama, he stood in silence by her bed and wrung his big hands until they were red. Finally, he whispered, "Mary, Mary."

"Yes, Simon," she answered softly.

"It——it's your Papa. Your Papa—he's—he's—gone."

The squeak of a mouse could have been heard as everyone waited for Mama's reaction. Slowly tears rolled down Mama's cheeks. Then she responded, "I'm too—sick to—grieve."

The following days and nights Papa sat beside Mama's bed to be of comfort to her. One evening she whispered to him, "Call the children to me."

Estella and Mabel came in and stood at the foot of the bed. Albert, holding Little John, was on the left side by her head. Papa entered the room and sat down on the low stool near her pillow, where he had sat many nights rubbing her back and arms trying to relieve her pain. His face was solemn, his eyes red and swollen. He said nothing. The only noise was Mother Mary's constant gasping for breath and the sniffing and occasional rustling of cloth as the children wiped their tears on their sleeves.

Suddenly, Papa lay his huge head over on Mama's bed and began sobbing like a baby. It tore the stillness to shreds. Mabel had never seen her papa act like that. He was big, brave, and strong.

Mama feebly stroked his bushy red hair. "Don't cry, Simon Pleasant— please don't cry—I'm going to a better place, where I'll never suffer again." Her voice was barely a whisper. Tears streamed from her eyes, wetting her pillow. She spoke again, oh so softly. Mabel thought she said, "You children help Papa —and do all you can to make each other happy——God will be with you 'through the valley of the shadow of——" Mama closed her eyes. "Live for God—and you can come—where I am going."

All was quiet for a long time. Then Estella announced, "I'm going to bed."

Mabel followed her. Estella was crying. When she calmed down, Mabel asked. "Where's Mama going?"

"You know," Estella snapped, "Now go to sleep and don't say another word."

Mabel was too scared to sleep. She could still hear Papa sobbing and hear an occasional mumble or groan from Mama.

Questions for reflection:

1. Why did Papa wish to move to Neosho?
2. What did Mama say when told that her father had died?
3. What was Mama's advice to the family?
4. Why was Papa having Mabel learn the verse about fearing no evil through the shadow of death?
5. How did each one in the family help the other?

When Mabel was older and traveled in this area, she changed trains at this station. There was a good spring of fresh water here. The Missouri and North Arkansas railroad lines met here. For this reason it was called Monark Springs.

This is Mabel's father, Simon Pleasant Andrew Kelley.

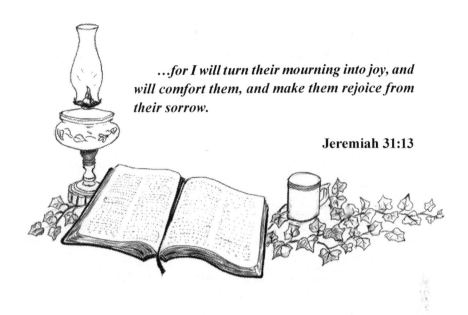

...for I will turn their mourning into joy, and will comfort them, and make them rejoice from their sorrow.

Jeremiah 31:13

MAMA GOES AWAY

Mabel awoke to sounds of people talking. She dressed and hurried into the big room where Mama stayed.

Mama wasn't coughing she was lying very still as if she were asleep. Mabel pulled a chair close to Mama and sat down in it. Mama didn't turn and look at Mabel, nor did she reach out to touch Mabel as she usually did, so Mabel waited for Mama to awake.

After a long wait, Mabel became irritated because each one in the room was speaking in low whispers. They were also walking on tiptoes as if they were afraid of awaking Mama. "Why don't they speak loudly and wake Mama so she will talk to us again?" Mabel asked Estella. Estella didn't answer. She just put her finger to her lips in silence, and kept wiping tears.

Mabel stomped into the kitchen. *What was going on? Why all these people? Why no breakfast?* She asked herself.

Later Uncle Albert and some strange men came bringing a big wooden box. They lifted Mama carefully, placing her in the big box and carried her out to his wagon. *What are you doing to my mama? Why don't you wake her up?* Mabel wanted to scream. Papa said nothing. He got into the wagon beside Mama and motioned for the children to get in.

Estella picked up Little John and said, "Come on, Mabel." Mabel followed obediently. When they were seated, Uncle Albert shook the reigns and shouted "Giddy-up!" The horse snorted a bit and began pulling the wagon away from the house.

"Where are we going?" Mabel whispered. No one answered. The neighbors followed in their wagons.

It was like a train of wagons. They went a long way until they came to a little white church. Behind the church, in a clearing among black jack oak trees, there were mounds and mounds of dirt. One was covered with crumpled dead flowers. Here and there white crosses were stuck in the dirt. Scattered among these were odd shaped gray rocks sticking up. Some had letters chiseled on the smooth sides of the rocks. Mabel had never seen such a strange place.

Uncle Albert slapped his horse with the long, leather strap and drove it right next to a mound of fresh dirt. Beside the mound of dirt was a big hole. When the wagon stopped, some women began singing about a beautiful home over there. Mabel wondered where that home was.

Then a man stood up and read from his Bible. *"Let not your heart be troubled: ye believe in God, believe also in me. In my Father's house are many mansions: if it were not so, I would have told you. I go to prepare a place for you... I will come again, and receive you unto myself; that where I am, there ye may be also."* Then he said, "Let us not sorrow for this loved one, for she is now enjoying her mansion. Prepare yourselves that you, too, may be accepted into a mansion when you die."

The next thing Mabel knew, the men had slipped ropes under the box and were lowering Mama down into the big hole. *No! No!* Mabel wanted to shout. *Don't do that! When my mama wakes, she won't be able to get out. Stop! Stop!* Nevertheless, Mabel had been taught that children do not give orders to adults. Besides, something was choking her and she could not speak. Also, deep in her heart, she knew that her mama would never wake again.

After the man prayed, the people began gathering around Papa and the children. Estella was holding Little John by one hand and Mabel by the other when an old man walked up and said, "I'm Cousin John Kelley, postmaster in Rocky Comfort. I need a girl just like you to come live with me." And he pulled Mabel away from Estella and wrapped his strange arms around her. Mabel wanted to run away, but then she knew she must not be rude to anyone, not even a stranger. "Now, what's your name?" he said, as he looked Mabel over. "My wife could really use you. Don't you want to come home with me?"

Another man who looked much like Papa said, "I'm Uncle Lon Kelley, I think Little John ought to be my boy now. My wife will take good care of him." He lifted Little John up in his arms.

"No," Papa said, "My family will stay together as long as I can manage. They need each other after their great loss."

An old lady pointed a bony finger at Papa and said, "Simon Pleasant Andrew Kelly, you were born a fighter. You came into the world the day the first gun was shot that started the Civil War. But how will you manage with four children and no wife? You surely don't plan on marrying again at your age, although you do look much younger than forty-five, no gray hairs; not even getting bald yet."

"We will make it somehow. God promised He will never leave us nor forsake us," Papa answered. "My faith is in God, not in myself."

She brushed a thin lock of white hair back from her face and shook her tiny head. Without saying another word, she walked away.

That night when they were all safe at home, Papa read Psalms 68:3-5, and said, "God says he will be a father to the fatherless, so He will surely be a mother to those without a mother. We can trust that God will always be with us and that we'll see Mary again if we obey God's commandments," he said. Mabel sure wanted to see her mama again, so when they bowed to pray, she asked Jesus to help her to always live to please Him.

A couple days later, Albert came home with Neosho's weekly newspaper. "Look, a write up about Mother Mary." He laid the paper on the table. Papa read it aloud.

The Times
Thursday, November 28, 1907.

Mrs. Mary Kelley, who lived on Grandma Crumbliss' farm, died Friday morning at 5 o'clock, and was buried at the Elliot cemetery at the Oak Wood church. The funeral service was conducted by James Cary. She leaves a husband and four children to mourn the loss. Mr. Kelley had just moved into this neighborhood in September and they were not very well acquainted around here. Mr. Kelley thanks the neighbors who showed their kindness at the last. Mrs. Kelley's father, who lived near the Goodman fruit farm was buried Friday, the day on which she died. Mrs. Kelley was a Christian woman.

After Mother Mary didn't need Papa anymore, he went back to teaching. Estella and Albert were also gone everyday, so Mabel was home caring for Little John. Every morning when Little John awoke he would go to Mama's bed and lay his head on it and cry. Mabel would hug him and pull him down on her lap and say, "Don't cry Little John, Mommy is gone to heaven where she don't hurt no more."

"But I want Mommy. Tell her to come back, Little John want her."

"Mama can't come back. We can go to her. Just be good boy and someday you will go see her. Okay?"

Little John was already sickly and coughed before Mother Mary died. Now as he cried for her day after day, he coughed more and ate less. Mabel's only way to comfort him was to tell him how she imagined heaven to be a wonderful place. He would then stop crying and say, "Me going to heaven."

"Good boy," Mabel answered.

Another year passed and still no school for Mabel, but she did not complain. She seemed content to be caring for Little John.

One day Estella said to Papa, "I can't understand why Mabel seems so happy."

Papa looked up from the book he was studying. "She's probably too young to understand."

"I think she does understand," remarked Albert, as he pulled off his boot. "Yesterday she was singing to that old rag doll, 'Our dear Mama, she's gone away; but I'm happy 'cause I'll see her someday.' "

"I go see Mommy, too," said Little John. Papa reached out his big hands and pulled Little John into his lap.

He wrapped his strong arms around Little John and said, "Yes, we will all see her sometime." Little John buried his face in Papa's bushy red whiskers. "God is keeping his promise to comfort us in our sorrow. Now I have two brides over yonder—Heaven never looked sweeter. Yes, God has been with us through the valley of the shadow of death. He will never leave us nor forsake us."

No one in the family thought much about Little John often saying that he was going to see Mama. Nevertheless, before another year passed, Little John was in heaven with her. It was almost more than Papa could bear. He said, "This place is too sad."

He moved the family near the Strawberry River in Arkansas.

Questions for reflection:

1. Whom did Papa trust to help him with his children?
2. Do you think talking about heaven helped Mabel?
3. Why do you think Mabel was content?
4. Can you remember one of the scriptures that helped the Kelley family?
5. Will God comfort us as he did the Kelley family?

The Edison School in Mangum, Oklahoma, built in 1909. This is where Mabel, at age twelve, entered school for the first time. Unless absent the day this picture was taken, she is in this picture.

Trust in the LORD, and do good... Delight thyself also in the LORD; and he shall give thee the desires of thine heart.

Psalms 37:3-4

MABEL GOES TO SCHOOL

"Are we almost to Mangum?" Mabel asked.

"I think we should soon be there," Papa said, as he straightened their boxes under their seats.

"Where'd yo'all come from?" asked the man in the seat across the aisle.

"We've come from Washington Township, Arkansas," Papa answered."

"Just you and yo'r girls? Where's yo'r woman?"

"I've had trouble with women. Had two, both died; little boy died, too. I do have an older son who stayed in Arkansas."

"Oh Papa," Mabel whispered hoping not to interrupt the conversation, "look at the flat green fields and cows everywhere. There must be some rich farmers to have so many cows."

"There is a rich rancher in Turkey Creek. They call 'em Jack. They say he owns 3,000 head. However, in this part of Oklahoma land is what we call open range country: the cows wander into any field and eat the grass. Several ranchers might own 'm cows you are seeing. One time each year, the cowboys from all the ranches have a round-up and brand 'em."

"Sir, may I ask how they know which cows belong to which rancher?" Mabel asked politely.

"Them calves stay close to 'ms mamas. She has a brand that was burned on her hip at a round-up before. So the cowboys brand the young cow the same as its mama."

Just then the train whistle blew. The train jerked and began slowing down. Black smoke billowed from the smoke stack and sparks flew into the air. Mabel screamed and jumped up to brush soot and sparks from her new dress. The man laughed. Then he raised his voice louder and continued talking, "Back about twenty years ago, a big part of the free range cattle froze to death."

"How did that happen?" Papa asked.

"Well, 'tus this way. Some ranchers got tired a haven' to go a way south to find their cattle for the spring round-up so they got together and built a long, tall fence to keep the cattle closer to home. That worked fine in mild winters. But that winter there was more snow than usual and it stayed frozen longer. The cattle went south to find grass but got stopped against the fence. There they huddled together trying to keep warm until they froze plum ta death."

"Oh, poor cows," Mabel said.

'Say, little girl, do you know what the cowboys used to call Mangum?"

"No, what?"

"They called it the *tin city* because so many tin cans were flattened and tacked on to cover the cracks in the walls. Of course, it ain't that way no more. Today it has many big perty buildun's and a three-story red brick courthouse, school building with three layers, a large church, and one of the most modern hospitals in Oklahoma. It was a *tin city* when herds of cattle (being driven from the south to the markets up north) passed on the trail near the city. But all that's changed too. The Long Island, Katy, and another railroad company saw the opportunity of haulen 'em cattle; so they built miles and miles of train tracks, and now they are carrying 'em cattle up north."

"Thanks for telling us about Magnum. I think we are going to like this place," Papa said.

"Much obliged, just wish to welcome you'ns."

When the Kelley family arrived in Magnum, they soon learned that the earlier settlers had become quite wealthy. There were many opportunities for work: being a "ranch hand" (even if you were not a cowboy) or serving as cooks or maids in the wealthy homes. Granite mines in the nearby hills also provided jobs. Many others worked at the large brick factory two miles north of town. Toward the southeast were the Quartz Mountains, where men could work cutting out quartz.

"I'm happy we came back to Oklahoma," Estella said, as they were arranging things in the little house Papa had rented.

"I'm glad; I'll get to go to school. I will, won't I Papa?"

"Yes, you should be able to start school."

Monday morning Mabel walked to the big brick school building in Mangum. The morning sun reflected off rows and rows of its tall windows. The rows of windows stood one on top of the other and another on top of that, and they covered every wall. Only rows of red brick separated the windows. They glistened in the sun like many huge stars. Mabel thought that Heaven must have buildings somewhat like the school building.

Papa had taught Mabel to read and write at home, but at last she was going to school. She had never been in such a large school building, nor seen so many students. It was so different from the schools where Papa had taught in Missouri. The year she had hoped to enter school (1906), the school at Pineville boasted three teachers and 145 students—more than it had ever had before.

Mabel looked around. Some girls were playing hopscotch, others jumping rope, other groups were laughing and talking. Boys were running everywhere chasing each other. Some were throwing balls, others shooting marbles. And from all directions other children were coming toward the school.

Mothers were holding the hand of their frightened little boy or girl. Mabel was eleven and large for her age. She shuddered with shame thinking she might be put in the classroom with these small beginning readers. Then Mabel noticed how afraid the little children were and thought how terrified they would be when their mothers must leave them. She said to herself, *just as God has been my comforter and helper, I will comfort and help these little children. I understand how it is to be lonely for your mother. I will not be a big dumb girl among little children. I will be their teacher's helper.*

Mabel loved to get to school early so she could have time to visit with her new friends. Even so, without a mother in the home, Mabel didn't always get up early enough to be at school early. Sometimes she arrived late, but Miss Perkins, the teacher, was kind when Mabel interrupted the lesson by entering late. Moreover, when Mabel played too much and then fell asleep without getting her homework finished, Miss Perkins scolded, but her eyes showed that she understood why Mabel's homework wasn't finished.

Mabel loved being at school, although at times she felt alone. The evening of the school program Mabel's heart was heavy. Papa had gone to see about a job and Stella was away for the evening. Albert had not moved with them to Mangum. Mabel's tears splashed into the wash pan as she thought of no one being there for her. Her friends' mothers were coming. Little John Smith's papa would be there for him, although he, too, had no mother. In her mind, she pictured how her mama might look sitting among the other women, smiling as Mabel recited her part.

After the kitchen was clean and the floor swept, Mabel hurriedly slipped into her clean dress, combed her hair and rushed away. As she entered the school, she saw Hope, dressed in a beautiful blue dress that her mother had made for this occasion. There was Bess, her black hair falling in ringlets to her waist. Her mother had arranged each one perfectly. Mary's mother was tying her sash in a beautiful bow.

"Hello, Mabel," the girls called cheerfully. Mabel tried to smile. Miss Perkins seemed to understand and asked Mabel to come and help her with some decorating. When they were alone, she said, "Mabel, I love your pretty smile. Keep smiling, but look, Honey, you must straighten your stockings, like this." And she began demonstrating how to pull on a stocking so every rib came straight up the leg.

Mabel bent over and straightened her stockings. *If only I had a mama, I'd know this already,* she thought.

As Miss Perkins rearranged Mabel's hair, she said, "Girls must take care about their clothes and keep their hair neat." When she finished, she kissed Mabel on the forehead, saying, "You look wonderful and I know you will do your part well."

Mabel smiled, she wasn't alone. She had Miss Perkins.

Questions for reflection:

1. How many years had Mabel waited to go to school?
2. Why did Mabel feel embarrassed?
3. Why did Mabel decide to help the little children?
4. Who helped Mabel not feel alone?
5. Try to think of sometime you have turned a bad situation into a good one.

For a long time, Papa didn't speak. When he could finally speak he pleaded, "Mabel, Mabel, my babe, don't take it so hard, please, please."

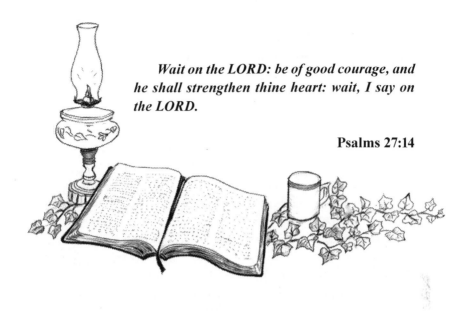

Wait on the LORD: be of good courage, and he shall strengthen thine heart: wait, I say on the LORD.

Psalms 27:14

PAPA GOES TO ARIZONA

One day when Mabel returned to her home after school, her brother was sitting in front of the house waiting to see her. "Albert!" she cried, throwing her arms around him.

Albert jumped up, held her out at arm's length, and looked her over. "Mabel, you've grown so much!" he gasped. "You're a young lady now. You must have had a good day. You look so happy."

"I'm happy 'cause you're here," she said as she squeezed him again. "You going to live here with us now?"

"No," he said, "It's this way. Our country is in a war right now. Our government is demanding all young men to fight. I've thought and prayed about this a long time. I love my country and want to help---but—I could never shoot a man, even an enemy. This last year I've been working hard raising food. I thought that would be helping our country, but the folks back home don't think so. They say I must go and fight like the other men. I think the authorities in this town think the same. As soon as they find out I'm in town, they'll also want to send me to the battlefield. I'd be useless if I wasn't going to shoot. So I've decided to go out west and hide way up in the mountains where no one can find me."

"But you will write to us?"

"Mabel, honey, if I write letters people will know where I am hiding."

"You will come back when the war is over, won't you?"

"Time will tell what will happen when the war is over. The way Papa moves around, you probably won't be here. But I will try to locate you."

"You mean I will never see you again?"

"No. No. I may have to change my name, but I can find you. Your name will always be Kelley, that is, until you marry. And the way you are growing, some guy will soon steal your heart." They both laughed.

"Oh, Albert, please promise me you'll be all right," Mabel pleaded, "and that we will see each other again."

Albert held Mabel's hand and said tenderly, "I wish I could promise that but—but—only God knows. Estelle and Papa are fixing a feast, so let's go eat it up. I'll be around for a few days."

When Albert was ready to leave, he hugged Papa first, then Estella, and then Mabel. Mabel clung to him a long time. He looked into her eyes and said, "Remember, if we never meet again on earth, we will meet in Heaven with Little John, Mother Mary and my mother."

That night before going to sleep, Mabel prayed, "Oh, God I know you are always with me, so I know You will also be with Albert."

The last few weeks, Mabel had been noticing a grave look on Papa's face. She thought he must be thinking about Albert and wondering if he was okay. Tonight he sat at the homemade desk, studying a map. Presently, he looked up and said, "Mabel, I must talk to you."

"Yes, Papa," she said as she hung up the skirt she had just finished pressing. She took the only other chair in the room and sat down facing him.

"The school term will soon be finished," he said. "I've just been thinking I may go west and see if I can locate another school for the fall term. I've read that the climate is dry there and that is better for folks with asthma. As you know, my asthma condition is worse since coming here. Perhaps I will feel better in the dryer climate. I am thinking of leaving as soon as school is out for the summer. That will give me time to find a job and a place for us to live before school starts again."

"Who will keep me? Estella stays at her job. I don't want to live alone."

"I've already arranged with Mrs. McNally to keep you. She is a nice woman and you already know her children. You can be her helper, for you are big and strong for a twelve-year old. Mrs. McNally says she'll be glad to give you a place to live in exchange for your help. They have a nice home, and you'll have her children to play with."

"Papa, Papa, I don't want you to leave," she said, beginning to cry.

"Neither do I want to leave, but I can't earn a living when I'm sick. Remember the Bible story about Samuel?" Papa said. "He was just a little boy and his mother took him to the temple and left him there. He did not get to see his mother for a year. I will send for you as soon as I find a place for us. Be brave like he was. Try to keep your mind on Jesus and you will not get so lonesome."

"Oh, Papa, Papa, please don't leave me." She laid her head on the desk. Her whole body shook as she sobbed. Clumsily, Papa fingered her long braids with his big hands. There wasn't a sound in the room, except for Mabel's sniffing and moaning.

For a long time, Papa didn't speak. When he could finally speak, he pleaded, "Mabel, Mabel, my babe, don't take it so hard, please, please. We won't be separated very long. God will be your father while I am gone. Psalms 10:14, says, *'Thou art the helper of the fatherless.'* Also remember your favorite verse, *'Weeping may endure for a night, but joy comes in the morning.'* Think about living in a nice warm country. They say it's warm in January and February and the sun shines all year round. Wouldn't you love to live where the sun shines every day?"

Without raising her head, Mabel said, "Yes, Papa, I'd love to live there with you. Please forgive me for being such a baby. It's just that I'll be so lonely. I still wish Mama and Little John were with us, although it has been such a long time . . . and Albert. Will I ever see Albert again? Estella is so busy with her job and her friends. She will not be coming home for weekends, so I won't ever get to be with her either."

"Your life will be different, but Estella has agreed to check on you and take you places. I'm sure you will be happy with the McNally children."

"Oh, Papa, Papa, please come back soon."

"Yes, yes, I will, my Babe."

"But I will miss you so-o-o. Papa, I love you." She flung her arms around his big broad shoulders and hid her face in his bushy red whiskers.

Papa lifted his steel blue eyes toward Heaven and then back to Mabel. He cleared his throat, then said, "Your crying has surprised me. You usually handle every problem so well; I must have thought you—you weren't human anymore—that you could smile through anything."

Mabel raised her head and looked at Papa. "Oh, Papa, Papa, I may never see you again." Then she started crying again.

"No Babe, no, I'll send for you as soon as I find a job and a place for us to live. Let me read you a verse." He took the Bible from the desk and with trembling hands turned to Isaiah 40:11. "*... he [God] shall gather the lambs with his arm, and carry them in his bosom...*' While I am away, God will take care of you. When you are sad, remember you are God's little lamb and he will take care of you. And read your Bible and be patient and you will see that God will keep his promises. You will find strength and comfort from reading it."

The following days were sad, but Mabel tried hard to act happy so Papa wouldn't feel so bad for leaving her. Papa bought his train ticket and packed his clothes. The night before he left, he took Mabel and her things to the McNally home. Mrs. McNally showed Mabel to her room and gave her a written list of what was expected of her.

Papa prayed with Mabel, kissed her good-bye, and disappeared into the darkness.

Questions for reflection:

1. Try to imagine how Mabel felt when her papa left her.
2. What would be your reaction if your father left you?
3. How old was Mabel?
4. Why couldn't Mabel stay with her mother?
5. What is Mabel's attitude toward her papa?
6. Do you think reading the Bible will help Mabel?

Mabel tended the garden, washed clothes, and did house work
for Mrs. McNally. She had no time to feel sorry for herself.

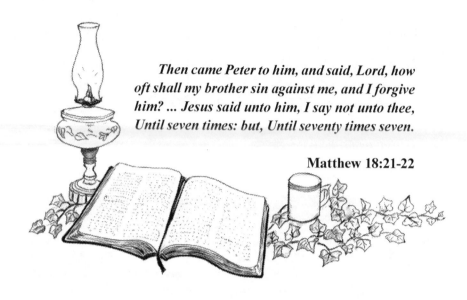

Then came Peter to him, and said, Lord, how oft shall my brother sin against me, and I forgive him? ... Jesus said unto him, I say not unto thee, Until seven times: but, Until seventy times seven.

Matthew 18:21-22

A SERVANT FOR MRS. MCNALLY

During the summer after Papa left, Mabel was working from early morning until night for Mrs. McNally. She found no time to feel sorry for herself, that is, except sometimes at night. Usually, though, she could hardly drag her weary legs up the stairs to her bedroom. Many times she fell asleep on her knees beside her cot. In the morning, before she felt rested, she could hear Mrs. McNally shouting harshly. "Get up, Sleepyhead! All you want to do is sleep. I think you would sleep yourself to death if I would let you. The beds are to be made. See, all the children are already out playing."

While the children played, Mabel straightened their beds. She swept and mopped floors that they dirtied. She baked the bread they ate, washed their clothes and mended their socks. She pulled weeds from the big garden that was to produce enough food to last all winter. She fed and watered the chickens.

Sometimes she would remember to take out her Bible and read the 13th chapter of 1st Corinthians. She learned quickly that reading the Bible helped her a great deal. She prayed, *Oh, dear Jesus, help me to be like it says in your book. Lord, I know I am supposed to be like you, but it seems*

I can't. I can't suffer long and be kind to the McNally children. They are so careless about dirtying up things that I have to clean. My fingers are hurting from scrubbing so many dresses today, and tomorrow I must do the boys' pants. They are so much harder to wash than dresses. Please God, make the boys be more careful with their clothes. And help me to suffer patiently. And, God, while you are working on them boys, make them stop walking with their muddy boots on the floors I just mopped.

Mabel tried hard every day to be cheerful, but it wasn't easy. The children spilled tomato soup on the white linen tablecloth that she had washed and ironed the day before. It could cost her an hour's work to put that tablecloth back on the table in the same condition that it was, just two minutes before they had carelessly spilled the soup.

Neither was it easy to be kind when Mrs. McNally criticized her for being slow. Mabel knew she was naturally slow, but didn't Mrs. McNally realize that being tired caused her to work more slowly?

Just this evening, Mrs. McNally had again scolded her about being so slow when washing dishes. "I've told you before not to take time to scrape all the food from the dishes before putting them into the dishwater. All those morsels of food make good slop for the pigs to eat. I'll say, Mabel, you don't even know how to make slop."

"I thought I was washing dishes, not making slop," Mabel murmured.

"What did you say?" Mrs. McNally demanded as she hurried out the door. She didn't wait for Mabel to repeat what she had said. Mabel was glad.

Estella had taught Mabel to scrape all the food out of the dishes before putting them in the clean soapy dishwater. That was how Mother Mary had taught her. However, Mrs. McNally wanted all the food in the water to make a good slop. Mabel often wondered how clean a dish could be when it emerged from a pan of *pig slop*. Anyway, to please Mrs. McNally she would wash dishes in slop water; nevertheless, in her and Papa's home she would always wash dishes in clean soapy water.

That evening as Mabel sat on the side of her bed she could hear the McNally boys wrestling in their room across the hall. *They still have plenty of energy,* she thought. *Maybe if they would help a little more with the work, I wouldn't be so tired and they wouldn't be so wild.* Betsy, the younger girl, was beating on the piano in the parlor below. Mabel thought she could make more music without having had a lesson than Betsy could after two years of lessons and practicing every day.

The Bible lay open on Mabel's lap. She was trying to make herself obey what she had just read. But the day had been hard. She read again, *Then came Peter to him, and said, 'Lord, how oft shall my brother sin against me and I forgive him?' ... Jesus said unto him, 'I say not unto thee, Until seven times: but, Until seventy times seven.'*

"Jesus," Mabel whispered, "that's impossible—that is—without Your help. Will You please help me? I want to obey Your Word so I can go to Heaven and see Mama and Little John, but I just can't have the right attitude for the McNally family unless You help me. Sometimes I can hardly forgive Papa for leaving me. And now that school is about to start again, I fear Mrs. McNally may keep me out to do the work. I do so want to go to school again."

Men nailed me on the cross. Then slashed open my side with a spear, Jesus seemed to answer.

They sure did, Mabel answered, *and You forgave them. Then I will try hard to forgive. Nobody's treated me that bad.*

And I will be with you and help you even to the end of the world, Jesus promised.

Mabel's attitude was different the following days. She was able to do her jobs easier and she went about her work singing.

A few days later, letters came from Papa. One was for her and one was for Mrs. McNally. Mabel thought the letter would be telling them that Papa had found a job and she would soon be leaving. She hurried up to her room, tore open the letter and read:

Dear Mabel,

I am in La Mesa, Arizona. It is a very nice town. New people from the East are coming here every day. I am feeling much better and have found a school in which to teach. There is only one sad thing about it. The town is very full and I cannot find a place suitable for us to live together. It breaks my heart to write this to you. I have written Mrs. McNally asking if she will keep you through the school year. If she cannot, I'm sure Estella will help you find a job for room and board at Mrs. Snodgrass' hotel downtown. I have also written Estella, explaining everything to her.

Love, Papa

Mabel let the letter fall to the floor. She wanted to scream, *Oh, Papa, my Papa, I so want to see you! I'm really tired working for Mrs. McNally. And Papa, Papa, if you only knew how I feel, you would send for me!*

She fell on her knees and began praying, *Oh, God, help me. Help me to be patient. Help Papa find a place for us. Please, Lord, please help us!* she cried.

Then she remembered again the verse Estella had read to her when Mother Mary was so sick. It had comforted her many times, so she found her Bible and read Psalms 30:5. *Weeping may endure for a night, but joy cometh in the morning,*

But this night has been so long. Oh, God, do please help me. Please take care of Papa, Albert, and Estella, and give me another place to live away from Mrs. McNally and her garden and her messy children. And thank You, God, for helping my attitude. Help me again. I know Jesus told Peter to forgive seven times —or was it more than that? Please, Lord, help me forgive.

Questions for reflection:

1. How would you feel if you had Mabel's problems?
2. In what ways did Mrs. McNally not treat Mabel fairly?
3. What should we do when people do not treat us fairly?
4. How did Mabel find the help she needed?
5. Does Mabel have normal attitude problems?
6. How many times was it that Jesus said we should forgive?

This church was constructed in 1910. It was near downtown where the hotels were in those years, so it is probably the one Mabel attended when she was allowed free time. It is one of the best preserved examples of early day church architecture in western Oklahoma.

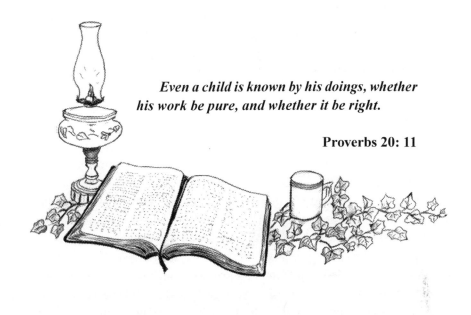

Even a child is known by his doings, whether his work be pure, and whether it be right.

Proverbs 20: 11

LIVING WITH MRS. SNODGRASS

Estella met Mabel after school and they went to the hotel to talk with the manager about finding Mabel a place to work in return for a place to live. The manager, Mrs. Snodgrass, seemed happy to have help. She said, "Your pay will be a place to sleep, your food, and a little spending money. You can attend school except on special occasions when I will need extra help."

"Except for Sundays when you need extra help, could Mabel have Sunday morning free to attend church?" Estella asked. "Our Papa wants us to attend as much as possible."

"Well, I suppose a little church wouldn't hurt anyone. However, looks as if God doesn't want churches in Mangum. At least not a Baptist church; 'em folks were meet'n in a half-dug out when there was jest a few of 'em. Then they had their doings in the jail, until a storm blew the jail away. Seems there was also another church blown away by a cyclone. Anyway, after that, 'em Baptist met in the schoolhouse while building their own chapel. Lighten struck that new chapel and it burned to the ground."

"Oh," Estella said in amazement.

Mrs. Snodgrass continued, "Now the First United Methodist folks have had better luck, maybe God likes 'em better. I don't know. There is that big, new red brick church down near the hospital. That would be a close one where Mabel might go. I'll let her go whenever I can."

"Thank you, Mrs. Snodgrass, thank you. And please be kind to my little sister," begged Estella. "She worked awfully hard at her other job."

"I'll do the best I can by her," answered Mrs. Snodgrass, "but she came here looking for work didn't she?"

And work she did. In the mornings before going to school, she helped prepare breakfast for the hotel guests. After school, she stripped each bed of soiled linens and replaced them with clean ones. She swept, mopped and dusted each room. When there was time before dark, she scrubbed the sheets, pillowcases, and towels on the old metal washboard out back of the hotel. Mabel's muscles were strong now, and the bed linens were easy in comparison to the muddy trousers of those McNally boys.

Guests at the Mangum Hotel had private rooms; but, for the workers, there were no private rooms. Mrs. Snodgrass and Mabel shared the hotel kitchen. Mabel's clothes, books, toothbrush, comb and trinkets were in a cardboard box tucked under her narrow bed. Her precious Bible was there, also. Each evening when it was possible, Mabel took it out and read in it. Since coming to the hotel, she had been reading the New Testament. She was trying to memorize Matthew 5:1-12, a part of Jesus' Sermon on the Mount. Today she was studying verse eight. *"Blessed are the pure in heart: for they shall see God."* She repeated the verse with her eyes closed, *"Blessed are the pure in heart: for they shall see God."* While her eyes were shut she prayed, *Father, please keep my heart pure so I can go to heaven and see Mama and Little John. And thank you, Jesus, that Mrs. Snodgrass is out, and I've had this quiet time with You today.*

People usually came in and went out of the kitchen from early morning until late in the evening. Mabel studied as she worked, or while Mrs. Snodgrass and her friends chattered loudly. If Mabel decided to look in the mirror, as all girls do, it was under the critical eyes of Mrs. Snodgrass. If Mabel felt sad, her tears fell in the audience of Mrs. Snodgrass, who often imagined Mabel had done something evil. Sometimes she scolded Mabel for things she imagined that Mabel had done.

These were problems, but none was equal to the problem of dressing. Very, very early in the mornings, old black Joe came to work. His first duty was to start a fire in the kitchen cook stove so it would be hot for cooking breakfast. Mabel tried hard to be up and dressed before Joe came. Sometimes, though, after working late in the evening or studying far into the night, she did not wake until old Joe was tapping at the door. On those mornings, she stayed under her quilt until he left the room.

This angered Mrs. Snodgrass. "I've never seen anyone as modest as you!" she would storm. "You are just plain fanatical to try and be so pure. If you had a rich dad, you might be that silly modest, but you don't. If you expect to make a liv'n working in hotels, you've got to be rough like all the hotel gang. Besides, who in the world would think it evil to dress in front of Old Joe?"

Joe went ahead with his work as if he hadn't heard.

Mabel covered her face with her quilt and prayed, *Lord, help me to continue to obey Papa and be modest. I know you want me to be that way, too. And please help Papa find a house so I can live with him.*

"Well, just lay there, lazy, little Miss Modest," Mrs. Snodgrass snickered. Suddenly, Mrs. Snodgrass stood up. Mabel held the quilt tight. She feared Mrs. Snodgrass might rip her quilt away. When she didn't, Mabel peeked through a hole in the quilt and saw that Mrs. Snodgrass was standing up pulling up her long stockings.

Wow! How indecent, Mabel thought.

When Old Joe left, Mabel got up and dressed.

Another problem while living with Mrs. Snodgrass in the hotel kitchen was that men (especially those a little tipsy after drinking whiskey) sometimes wandered into the kitchen after Mabel had gone to bed. Usually Mrs. Snodgrass shooed them out. At times, however, when Mrs. Snodgrass wanted money, Mabel thought she was tempted to let the men get in bed with her.

Mabel liked Old Joe. He whistled while he worked. Sometimes she recognized the tunes to be hymns. She liked him for other reasons too. He spoke kindly to her. Whenever he could, he pumped the water from the well and filled the big tubs where Mabel washed and rinsed the clothes. He also helped her dump the heavy tubs of dirty, soapy water. Yet sometimes other jobs kept him too busy. Then Mabel had to dump the tubs of dirty water and refill them with water she drew from the well. This made her workload doubly hard.

One day when Mabel was walking home from school, she met Old Joe. "Hey, ye girl," he said rather softly. "Hey, you, Mabel, want to talk to ye."

Mabel answered respectfully, "Yes, sir," as Papa had taught her, although Mabel knew that white folks were not friendly to Blacks. They only spoke with Blacks to tell them some job to do.

"Say, girl, I jest wants to say, you good girl. Don't you do what dat Mrs. Snodgrass tell you. She no good woman. You good girl. You jest stay good like you is and dee good Lord, He will bless ye. I been want'n tu tell you this fer a long time, but I dare not get Mrs. Snodgrass angry. Old Joe can't afford to lose his job. Dat's all I have tu say." He tottered on down the road.

Humm, the Bible says, Even a child is known by his doings whether his work be pure and whether it be right, Mabel said to herself.

That night when Mabel prayed, she repeated again the verse she was learning, *"Blessed are the pure in heart: for they shall see God."* Then she prayed, *God, make my heart and mind pure as I keep my body pure. It seems somewhat dirty when I get angry or feel sorry for myself.*

Questions for reflection:

1. In what ways was living at the hotel different from living with the McNallys?
2. What were some of Mabel's problems while living at the hotel?
3. Was it hard for Mabel to pray and read her Bible in the hotel kitchen?
4. How did Mabel show that she loved Jesus?
5. What did Old Joe and Papa want Mabel to do?

Mabel cleaned hotel rooms and washed the linens
after school and on Saturdays and Sundays.

It is good that a man should both hope and quietly wait for the salvation of the Lord.

Lamentations 3:26

A NEW PLAN

Before going to bed, Mabel opened her Bible and read, *It is good that a man should both hope and quietly wait for the salvation of the Lord.* As she lay awake thinking of the promise in this verse, she began hoping and dreaming of seeing Papa and Albert again. Her salvation from God would be to get away from the hotel and be with them. Slowly a wonderful new plan came to her. She could hardly wait to tell Estella and asked her opinion about the idea.

Early the following morning she said to Mrs. Snodgrass, "May I have a day off next week? I'm having my sixteenth birthday and Estella asked me to spend the day with her."

"Well, yes, you can," she answered gruffly. "Just be sure you're back before I go tu bed, so I won't have to git out of bed and open the door fer you."

Estella came for Mabel the morning of her birthday. "Let's go to the photographer first," she said. "This is a special day. Better have your picture made while you are young and pretty. Put on your new white dress; and here," then opening the sack in her hand, she continued, "I brought you a bow for your hair."

Mabel wanted to hurry away and talk over her new plans. However, she obediently changed into her new white dress and put the large white bow in her hair.

"Estella, have you gotten a letter from Henry Albert or Papa recently?" Mabel asked as they were leaving the hotel.

"No, why do you ask?"

"Papa is in Oklahoma City! Look, I have a letter."

It bore the stamp of Oklahoma City, OK, Sept. 1916. Although Mabel had read the letter many times, she started reading it to Estella as they walked along the brick sidewalk.

> *Oklahoma City*
>
> *Sept. 12, 1916*
>
> *Mabel, dear child,*
>
> *You don't know how I have longed to hear from you. I received your letter this morning. I was very glad to hear from you. Oh! Mabel, if you knew how much pleasure it gives me to hear from you, you would write me often—*

"Careful! You're about to run into a tree," shouted Estella, as she jerked Mabel's arm. "Whoops," Mabel stepped aside but continued reading.

> *I have been going to meeting almost every night since I came here. I have been to the Pentecostal, the Salvation Army, the Peoples Mission, and the Church of God. They all preach holiness.*

"Watch out! Mabel, there is a hole in the sidewalk. Now look Mabel, let's just stand here until you are finished reading or you are going to hurt yourself."

"Okay," Mabel answered. She stopped and leaned against a tree, then she continued reading.

> *I suppose I lost my pocket book in a theater the second night I was in this city. I have not been in another since and*

don't want to go in. My heart is turned against all worldly pleasure.

I am in a trial, but the Lord has given me consolation and power. I promised Him if He would help me overcome a certain sin, I would preach His gospel and I have great faith that He is carrying me through with victory. Yes, praise His holy name! Sunday evening I got so near to heaven I almost said, 'Glory to God!' The Lord is working with me wonderfully. I think the Lord will carry me through.

Mabel, I think the Lord wants you to get an education to His glory. Don't think of anything but to glorify God and He will make a way for us. Oh! that you might be a poet to the glory of God and write songs to praise him. Oh! I do like poetry so much.

I haven't earned a dollar since I came here. I lost over five dollars, and I have got my board on credit since I've been here.

Mabel, quit everything that comes between you and God, and He will lead you in all truth. When you don't know whether to do something or not, ask yourself if Jesus was here would He do that? He will, through your conscience, say, 'yes, or no.' Now do that Mabel, will you? And if you have done anything that has separated you from Him, confess you have sinned and ask Him to forgive you, and do it no more by the help of His power. Pray earnestly that you may know the things that are not pleasing in His sight and ask Him to help you overcome everything that is sinful and unclean.

Oh, Mabel, do you think of a home where we could be together? Make your request known to God. You know one time the Savior said, "The foxes have holes and the birds have nests but the son of man has not where to lay his head." I think of the loving Savior without a home.

First seek the kingdom of God and His righteousness and these things will be added to you. "Oh, think of a home over there, by the side of the River of Life. The saints all immortal and fair are robed in their garments of white." (Quoted from a song.) He has gone to prepare a mansion there where we will be with him and your mama and Little John and all those that have gone on before.

Although I am abounding in love, I have not got the witness of full salvation; but I am determined to go on. May the Lord bless you and establish your heart in His love, My prayer is for you.

I will send a money order or a check for $5.00 dollars... while working as I can this winter. Don't be discouraged, and go on studying all you can.

Mabel, read the Bible every day, and pray that the Lord may keep you from evil. Be kind to everybody, and go to church; remember it pleases God. Write to me and be careful in school and everything and try to do your work nicely.

Good bye, my Baby,

Papa

"Isn't that exciting? Papa is so close to us. Let's go see him!" Mabel said, while she folded the letter and tucked it safely into her pocket.

"Maybe you can, but I have a good job and I don't want to leave Wallace," Estella answered.

"Estella, I have just one thought in mind and that is to go be with Papa," Mabel said boldly. "Don't you think that would be good? Mrs. Snodgrass has been giving me a little more money this summer now that I'm helping her all day instead of attending school."

"But Mabel," Estella said in surprise, "Oklahoma City is a big, big city. And since it has become the capital of Oklahoma, it is growing every day. I don't think you could find him among thousands of strangers!"

"I have the street name and the house number. What more do I need? I think I have enough money to buy my ticket. Shall we go to the train station today and see how much it will cost?"

"First, we have to get your picture taken. Then we can go to the train station and find out what you will need to know—if there is a railroad that runs from here to Oklahoma City? We are a way out west. We are nearer to Texas than to Oklahoma City."

As they were walking home, Estella spoke very seriously, "Mabel, I think it dangerous for you to go hunting for Papa. Surely Papa will come for you when he has a place for you."

"I'm sixteen, plenty old enough to travel by myself. I'm not the little girl he left four years ago."

"Another thing to consider is that winter is coming soon. There aren't as many jobs in the winter, but always added expenses: buying warm clothes, heavy shoes and fuel to keep a place warm. It might be wise if you stayed here at least until spring. You would have a better chance of getting a job and could get more prepared for winter when it comes again."

"But I want to see Papa," Mabel protested. "I think I could cook for him and he might get well."

"I'm sure you could help him."

"Albert Henry might come back any time, too. He could help me find Papa."

"I really think you should wait until spring. If Henry comes he could go with you."

"Maybe I should be more patient. The Bible verse I read this morning said that it was 'good for a man to hope and quietly wait for the salvation of the Lord.' I guess God was telling me to take your advice and wait. Isn't it strange how God lets us read just what we need for the day?"

"Yes, God is good to help us every day. When you do leave, remember to write to me."

"I will write," Mabel promised.

The day passed so quickly that Mabel forgot Mrs. Snodgrass' command to be home before she went to bed. Mrs. Snodgrass was angry when she had to get out of bed and open the door. "Now look here, little Miss Modest," she said angrily. "I know you act so pious and goodie around here, but I'll bet you have been out with your lover. You were probably so cozy in his arms you just couldn't break—away."

Mabel clutched her chest as if she'd been stabbed with a knife. Because she wanted to be pure more than anything else, she preferred a whipping rather than to be accused of something like that. Far into the night while Mrs. Snodgrass was snoring, Mabel cried and prayed. The longer she cried, the more she wanted to be away from Mrs. Snodgrass and with her caring Papa. She repeated the verse she had read that morning, over and over again to herself, until she went to sleep. *It is good that a man should both hope and quietly wait for the salvation of the Lord.*

When Mrs. Snodgrass' anger had cooled, Mabel told her that she wanted to go in the spring to Oklahoma City to look for her papa and that she would not go to school so she could earn money for her trip.

Mrs. Snodgrass never said a word, she just nodded, "Yes."

Each Sunday, unless a big snow was on the ground, Mabel hurried through her morning's work and went to church. She wanted to do what Jesus wanted as Papa had advised her to do.

Mabel worked hard all that winter. It seemed so long; and when spring finally came, Mabel counted her money. She had enough for her ticket, so she said to Mrs. Snodgrass, "I'm going to Oklahoma City to find my Papa."

Mrs. Snodgrass' answer was, "I know why you are leaving. Gotta baby on the way and want to hide away. You can tell strangers you're a widow, and won't be so embarrassing. I noticed you are getting fat. I guess I was right about why ye stayed out so late that night."

Mabel felt she couldn't take another accusation from Mrs. Snodgrass. She burst out crying and said, "You know I'm not that kind of girl."

"Don't feel so bad," Mrs. Snodgrass said with a tiny tone of comfort in her voice. "It happens to lots of girl that have to earn their living working in hotels."

Questions for reflection:

1. What were two goals that Mabel had for herself?
2. What were two things Papa wanted Mabel to do?
3. Why did Estella advise Mabel to wait until spring?
4. What verse had God given that morning?
5. Name two things Mabel want to do?

Santa Fe Railroad depot in Oklahoma City, Oklahoma, around 1910.

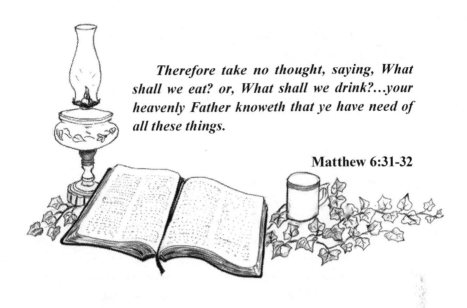

Therefore take no thought, saying, What shall we eat? or, What shall we drink?...your heavenly Father knoweth that ye have need of all these things.

Matthew 6:31-32

WHERE IS PAPA?

Mabel sang while packing her clothes and her few belongings into an old suitcase. At last she was leaving Mangum and heading to Oklahoma City and to her beloved Papa. Mrs. Snodgrass was out in the hotel lobby attending to a guest, so Mabel fell to her knees beside the cot where she had slept for the past three years. *Thank you, Jesus,* she said, *for keeping me pure and safe and for helping me have a right attitude toward Mrs. Snodgrass. Thank you that I feel thankful to her for keeping me here. I could have been out on the street without a place to sleep. Thank you that I'm leaving without shame. You are to be praised.* Then she opened her New Testament and read her verse for the day, *'Therefore take no thought, saying, What shall we eat? or, What shall we drink? . . .Your heavenly Father knoweth that ye have need of all these things.'*

"Yes, Jesus, I know you will take care of me until I am safe with Papa. I love You, Jesus," Mabel prayed

Estella and her friend, Wallace, came to tell Mabel bye. Wallace came for her old suitcase and carried it to the train station. Mabel felt both happy and sad. The day was both bitter and sweet. She found it hard to leave the hotel and Mrs. Snodgrass, although she felt happy to be leaving. What strange feelings welled up within her, she felt sad leaving her sister, yet happy to be going to see Papa.

She leaned out the train window and waved to Estella and Wallace, while tears streamed down her face. She could see Estella wiping her eyes and Wallace was trying to comfort her. It might be the last time the sisters would see each other. However, Mabel had a mission to do. She must take the risk, whatever risk it might be to find her papa. She needed Papa, and she felt Papa needed her.

Mabel arrived in Oklahoma City the following morning. When she saw multitudes of people scurrying in all directions, the massive buildings towering overhead, and the cars and trains whizzing by, she remembered Estella's warning that the city was too large for her to find Papa. *How true Estella was*, Mabel thought. Then she whispered a prayer, *Lord, please help me. I have no one to depend on but You.* To gain courage, Mabel repeated, a Bible verse found in Philippians 4:13, *I can do all things through Christ which strengthens me.*

She saw people getting on a little train so she hopped on too. "Does this train go to 12th street?" she asked.

"Yes," the driver informed her. With a little help from the driver, Mabel found the address on the letter she had received from Papa. She thought she would quickly find him. However, he had moved away from that house and the manager in charge didn't know where he had gone. Mabel dragged and carried her heavy suitcase from apartment house to apartment house searching for Papa until she thought she couldn't take another step. She found a large tree in a secluded place, took her Bible out of her suitcase, and sat down on the suitcase.

Mabel wanted to cry, but she had learned that crying didn't help; however, praying and reading her Bible did. So she prayed: *Dear Jesus, the day is gone, it will soon be dark and I have no idea as to where Papa is. And I have no money for a hotel. Estella warned me that Papa would be hard to find in this large city among so many people. Oklahoma City is so different from Mangum. God help me know what to do. I have no money to return to Mangum.* Then she opened her Bible to Matthew 6:31-32 where she had read before leaving the hotel yesterday. *". . .take no thought, saying, What shall we eat? or, What shall we drink?. . .your heavenly Father knows that ye have need of all these things."* But, Jesus, I'm afraid. What will I do? Where will I stay during the long dark night?

Then she thought of the train depot. She put her Bible away and trudged back to the train station and sat wearily down on the bench.

The next thing she knew, she was waking up and the ticket agent was announcing over the speaker, "The station will be closing in five minutes. There are no more arrivals or departures tonight."

Mabel jumped up and ran to the agent. "I'm not waiting for a train. It's just that I—that—I— have no place to go. I came looking for my papa, but I haven't found him yet."

"Sorry," he said. "If we allowed people to spend the night here, it'd be full every evening. You're just one among the hundreds of new people coming every day. There are lots of others who have no place to stay. Why didn't you bring money for a hotel?"

"I had none left after buying my ticket."

"I'm sorry," he said.

Mabel dragged her suitcase out into the dark night. Although the evening was not cold, Mabel shivered in the darkness as she heard the door of the train depot locking shut behind her. She leaned against the depot window and murmured, *I wish I were back in Mangum. Being with Mrs. Snodgrass isn't as bad as this.*

A few minutes later a man walked by and looked her over. Trembling, Mabel hurriedly picked up her suitcase and started walking as if she had somewhere to go. As soon as he was out of sight and the street was again empty, she sat her weary body down on her suitcase again.

To encourage herself, Mabel tried to repeat the Bible verse she had read before she returned to the station. *Don't worry about what you will eat or what you will wear. God will take care of you. Well, it was something like that,* she said to herself; and then she began repeating other verses she had memorized: *The Lord is my shepherd, I shall not want. Estella taught me that verse before Mama died. I will keep him in perfect peace whose mind is stayed on Me. But how can I keep my mind on God when I am hungry and there are so many things to fear?* she questioned. And then she remembered, *what time I am afraid, I will trust in thee.* And then, *I will turn their mourning into joy, and comfort them. Wow! How much better I feel.* And then she quoted to herself the one that had kept her going all day. Philippians 4:13, *I can do all things through Christ who strengthens me.*

Mabel was standing directly under the streetlight,
repeating to herself portions of the Bible, when Mr.
Martin, the police officer, made his nightly rounds.

Mabel was standing directly under the streetlight, repeating to herself portions of the Bible, when Mr. Martin, the police officer, made his nightly rounds. He looked very sternly at Mabel, so she jumped to her feet and started walking again, pretending she was going to her home. Mabel knew people were not to be out on the city streets late at night. But where else could she be? Before long, Mr. Martin came back down the street. Mabel wanted to duck into an alley and hide, but it was too late. Before long, he came again. Mabel wondered if he could be trusted. She knew some of the police officers who came into the Mangum hotel were not to be trusted. *Oh, my Father in Heaven,* she prayed, *please protect me.*

Mabel watched as Mr. Martin turned around and headed back to her. She jumped to her feet and faced him. By now she knew that he knew she was going nowhere.

"Hey, there, gal," he shouted gruffly. "Who you wait'n fur? You better get on home to your pappy." Mabel just stood there, thinking how she'd love to do just that. "I said to go on home!" he demanded with sternness.

Mabel was trembling. She could feel her heart racing. She clutched her jacket as if to stop her heart from running away. For a moment, she could not speak or move.

"So you're not going home, then I'll take care of you, you run-away," he ordered. "I'll take you to the police chief and see what he wants to do with ye."

Mabel still could not speak. Her heart was still racing, her breath short and shallow.

"What's your name?" the policeman barked.

"Mabel May Kelley," she whispered.

He wrote in his book, and then asked, "Why aren't you at home?"

When she got control of herself enough to speak, Mabel said, "I came here just today. I'm looking for my papa. I have a letter saying where he was living. I found the house, but the people told me he had moved."

"Let me see that letter," he demanded, "probably from your feller."

Mabel took out her precious letter and handed it to him. "Oh, Sir, I don't have a feller. That letter is from my papa, and please, Sir, will you give it back after you've read it. That's all I have of my papa's."

"Where's your mama?"

"She died nine years ago."

"No brothers or sisters?"

"I have one sister in Mangum and a brother who disappeared."

"I've heard stories like that before," he said bluntly. He read her letter. "Why did he call you baby if he is your Papa?"

"I'm his youngest living child."

"I've heard a lot of stories. This one beats them all. Why did your beloved Papa leave his little baby alone and come here?"

"My papa has asthma and had to move to a dry climate. He didn't leave me alone. He left me with Mrs. McNally."

Mr. Martin said no more. After what seemed a long time, he spoke slowly, "For some reason I believe your story. I think I will take you to my home. My wife is looking for a girl to help with our housework. Finding your papa in Oklahoma City may take a long time. There are more than 90,000 people in this city."

Mabel caught her breath. Was she hearing right or was she dreaming? Where would Papa be among so many?

"If my wife is satisfied with your work, you'll have a place to stay until we find your papa." He smiled and nodded his head.

Mabel wanted to shout, 'Thank you,' 'Thank you' a hundred times, but a lump in her throat kept her from speaking. She cleared her throat and whispered, "Oh, thank you, Sir. Thank you. I'll do the best that I can. Mrs. McNally and Mrs. Snodgrass taught me to clean and wash clothes."

"Stay right there; I'll be right back and take you to our home." He roared away on his motorcycle.

Tears of thanksgiving rolled down Mabel's cheeks and fell on her white dress. It was the first time she had noticed how dirty her dress was. *I put it on clean when I left Mangum.* Mabel drew in a deep breath, and the verse *'Weeping may endure for a night but joy comes in the morning'* came to her mind. *So much has happened, seems like it has been a week since I waved good-bye to Estella and Wallace yesterday.*

Questions for reflection:

1. What verse did Mabel read in the morning?
2. What did Mabel do when she was discouraged?
3. Can you repeat a verse that Mabel memorized?
4. Why did Mr. Martin take Mabel to his home?
5. Do you think God caused Mr. Martin to help Mabel?

Mabel was happy helping Mrs. Martin.

Hold thou me up, and I shall be safe: and I will have respect unto thy statutes continually.

Psalms 119:117

NEW HOPE

Every day while Mabel helped Mrs. Martin keep their home clean, her husband, Officer Martin, was looking for Mabel's papa, Simon Pleasant Andrew Kelley.

Mrs. Martin had just given birth to another baby. Mabel sang as she did the house work and washed their clothes. She thanked God every day for having a home; and as she cleaned the Martin's home, she was dreaming of the day when she would be cleaning house for her beloved Papa.

Nevertheless, after weeks passed and not a trace of Papa, loneliness and fear ate away at her faith. Thoughts that Papa had moved back to Arizona haunted her at night when she tried to sleep. At times when she was extremely sad, God helped her remember His promise, *"I will never leave thee nor forsake thee." Yes, Jesus you have been with me through all these four years. You have held me up and I shall respect and obey your commandments forever,* Mabel prayed.

One day she heard Mr. Martin ask, "Had any trouble with Mabel? She seems to be responsible."

"She is a really good helper, but the thing I like most is her admirable character," answered Mrs. Martin. "She never gets angry or pouts when I correct her. She says that she has never taken a drink of beer nor smoked a cigarette. That's unusual for youngsters left alone."

"That's right," continued Mr. Martin. "And I have never heard her speak a bad word or even slang, and I'm sure she's had to work around people saying bad words. Think she is a Christian?"

"Yes, I do. She sings a lot of hymns while working. You know, I've just been thinking that maybe going to church would keep her from being so lonely. She must have learned the hymns in church. Maybe, too, she could find some friends."

"Maybe she might meet someone else who needs help in their home. We can't keep her forever. You know, I feel bad that I thought she was a rebel that night when I picked her up."

"She could have been; one never knows when they see someone out on the street at night. But do you have any leads on her Papa? The poor girl really longs for him."

"I've found a place he had been working, but they said he quit because of illness."

"Maybe you could trace him through medical records," Mrs. Martin suggested. "And shall we let her be away on Sundays so she can go to church and find some friends?"

"Yes, I think it would be good. I'll try to find some church addresses for her. She seems to know how to ride the street cars and find places in the city."

"Oh, yes, she does a lot of my shopping."

The following Sunday Mabel set out to find a church. Papa had said he went to the Salvation Army, the Pentecostal, The People's Mission and the Church of God. The Church of God sounded best to Mabel. Somewhere in her memory she thought they had attended a Church of God, maybe in Neosho or in Arkansas. She found the address that Mr. Martin had given her of one on Capitol Hill. She arrived while the congregation was singing. The songs were different from the church she had attended in Mangum, but they also seemed distantly familiar.

After the service was dismissed, a group of people gathered around and introduced themselves. Among them were Elsie Egermeier, Mrs. Hunter, and Lou Hightower and her sons. Mabel remembered one attractive son was named Alvin. She walked away from the little church with mixed feelings. She was very disappointed that Papa hadn't been there, although worshiping God with others lifted her spirit and meeting new people was exciting.

Although her hopes to find Papa were sometimes high and sometimes very low, the church service had encouraged her to continue believing that she *could do all things through Christ,* even find her Papa. All the way to the church and back to the Martin's home, Mabel had looked for Papa, just as she did each time she went to the market to buy things for Mrs. Martin. Sometimes she was sure she saw Papa and her heart would skip a beat. But when she looked more carefully, she knew it wasn't him.

A few weeks later, after Mrs. Martin was strong enough to do her own housework, Mabel heard her ask her husband, "Found any traces of Mabel's papa?"

"Nothing secure," he answered.

"Seems that he would have visited a doctor when he was sick. You suppose he died?"

Mabel shuddered at the thought. She listened more carefully.

"I've checked, but found no death recorded for a Mr. Kelley."

"Well, what will we do? I wish I could keep Mabel forever, but we can't afford it."

"I'll try to find her another job," said Mr. Martin.

It wasn't long until Mabel had a new day job. It was with Mrs. Lou Hightower, one of the women she had met at the church.

The arrangements were made: Mabel would work and eat her meals at the Hightower's and sleep at the Martin's home.

The Hightower family lived at 2806 S. Robinson in Oklahoma City. Mrs. Lou Ellen Hightower helped with family expenses by keeping boarders. The boarders ate and slept at the Hightower home for a fee. Besides cooking and cleaning for these men, Mrs. Hightower had four boys of her own, ranging in ages from 5 to 26 years.

Mrs. Hightower needed Mabel's help, with three and sometimes four boarders and a family of six. They ate an astonishing amount of food each day. It was much like cooking and cleaning at the hotel in Mangum. That is, except Mrs. Hightower seemed very different from Mrs. Snodgrass.

Mabel had never known a family in which everyone had freckles and different shades of red hair. Alvin, the oldest, had sandy red hair; Cornelius a little more red; James Ezra's hair was fiery red; and Aubrey's a dark auburn red—much darker than that of his mother. Mr. Hightower's hair was light brown.

Alvin was 26, the same age as Mabel's brother, Albert. He had lovely blue eyes. Mabel thought she would like to be his friend. He, Mr. Hightower, and 18-year-old Cornelius worked at the Wilson Meat Packing house. Each week when Alvin was paid, he brought his money home and gave his mother all she needed.

Mr. James Hightower was 55 years old and not well. When he was only 17 years old, his father died, leaving the children without either parent. Before his father died, Mr. James Hightower promised his father to keep his siblings together as a family. He had ruined his health operating a farm many years in order to care for these siblings. Eleven years later, when he married Miss Lou, two sisters and a brother were still living with him.

Mrs. Lou was 44 years old, a little shorter than Mabel, and near 50 pounds lighter. She scurried around the house like a tiny mouse. "Here, peel these potatoes," she would say pushing a dishpan full of potatoes in front of Mabel, then she'd rush away to do another job.

Questions for reflection:

1. What verse gave Mabel hope?
2. Why did Mrs. Martin think Mabel was a Christian?
3. What did Mrs. Martin like best about Mabel?
4. Why did Mabel believe she would find Papa?
5. Will Mabel be happy working for Mrs. Hightower? Why?

Mabel and friends in Oklahoma City

O that there was such a heart in them, that they would fear me, and keep all my commandments always, that it might be well with them, and withtheir children for ever!

Deuteronomy 5:29

A NEW JOB AND NEW FRIENDS

Mrs. Lou Hightower was a Christian woman, but very moody. When Mabel came to work each morning, she never knew what mood Mrs. Lou would be in. Would she be in a happy, sad, hasty, or "a feel sorry for me" mood?

One day when she was in a talkative mood, she said to Mabel, "I hear your mother died; then your papa left you and you came here looking for him."

"Yes, madam," Mabel answered.

"At least you know your papa loves you."

"Yes, madam," Mabel said again.

"Let me tell you about my pap," she said as she was mixing bread. Mabel was cleaning. Mrs. Lou showed her how to take ashes from the wood burning cook-stove and rub them on the outside of the pots to clean them. This took a long time; so as she was cleaning the many big pots that Mrs. Lou used for cooking, she listened to Mrs. Lou.

"One day when I was three or four years old, my pappy packed his things and said, 'I'm going to look for work. I followed him out to the wagon and begged to go. He lifted me in his arms and kissed me good-bye, saying, 'Run in the house. When I find a job, I'll come and get you.' That's the last time I saw him. I don't think he loved his family."

"Oh, I know my papa loves me," Mabel assured her.

As if Mabel hadn't said a word, Mrs. Lou continued. "He wrote to Mama just once. Mama found out about a year later that he had left the country with another woman. We were staying with my pappy's mother, my Grandma Sharp. How well I remember seeing my mama walking the floor and crying. My brother James was six months old, I think. Mama was hardly able to work, but she started going from house to house asking for clothes to wash or ironing to do, or for sewing. She worked almost day and night to earn enough to buy what we needed. I took care of little Jimmy."

"I'm so sorry," Mabel said politely, but Mrs. Lou kept on talking.

"These women today can find jobs in the packing houses, telephone companies, hotels, offices, and bakeries. *(Mabel noted all the places she might find a job.)* T'was different in those days, there was mostly only servant work for women. Mama worked hard, and soon we moved into a house of our own.

"My brother Pete, four years older than myself, worked too, caring for the neighbors' animals, weeding in their gardens, and shoveling coal." Suddenly, she threw back her head and laughed. "Sometimes he'd come home looking like a little 'black boy' cause he'd be black all over. We had a little lean-to room on the side of the house. Mama would make him stay in that room 'till he washed and changed clothes so the coal dust wouldn't get on the clean laundry she'd just washed and folded."

As they continued working, Mabel said, "Tell me more about your childhood; why didn't your mother's family help her?"

"We lived in Arkansas; her family lived far away in Alabama. She never had enough money to return to her family."

"Our family lived in Washington Township, Independence county Arkansas when I was 10 years old," Mabel said. "Is that near where you lived?"

"We lived in Izard County. Independence and Izard county are side by side. The love of my life, Mr. Hightower, also lived there. He lived right next door to my mother. But I never met him until I was 15 and he was 26 years old."

"Why didn't you meet him, if he lived next door?"

Mrs. Lou had a far-away look in her eyes. "It's a long story," she sighed.

But I will tell you. You may relate to what has happened to me. When I was about five years old, Mother was so sick that neither she nor Doctor Morris thought she could live.

Old Doctor Morris came one day with his wife and asked Mother about her family and what would happen to us children if she died. Because mother had no family near, she let the Morris family take me home with them. They thought the boys, Peter, then twelve, and little Jimmy could take care of themselves better than I.

Mabel couldn't imagine a mother giving her child away.

Mother was wise in what she did. Doc. and Mom Morris were like loving grandparents to me. Living with them, I had time to play and study as all children should do. At first, I was so lonely I could hardly eat, and often I would go down in the orchard and have a good cry. Then I would feel better. I played with their two-year-old grandson, Little Johnny, which kept me from missing my little brother so badly. Their son, George, my age, also played with me and taught me to ride the horses. The only trouble I had was when Mom Morris made George and me sit down and study. When she taught us how to spell, I would yawn and try to go to sleep; yet she kept after me until I got it. In the winter, we went to school together.

Mom Morris kept us busy in the summer time. The hens would hide their nests out in the bushes so we couldn't rob their eggs. When Mom Morris needed eggs, we had to find a nest. When we found a nest of eggs, she would come, feel the eggs, and take only the warm one. If the egg was warm, it was fresh. Sometimes the hens would surprise us with a brood of newly hatched, fluffy, yellow chicks.

Doctor Morris kept beautiful flower and vegetable gardens. We helped him pick the squash, beans, and strawberries. We picked apples and peaches, washed and split them open. Then we dusted them with a little sulfur powder, carried them up to the roof, and laid them out to dry. Oh, Joy! Prancing around on the roof was delightful. We ate all the while we worked. It is surprising how much freshly picked fruit a child can hold.

Five years later (when I was ten), my mother came to get me. But she did not seem like my mother. I had not seen any of my family for five long years, and I was so happy in my new home that I didn't want to go. She understood, although I'm sure it hurt her deeply.

Mrs. Lou wiped a tear from her cheek. Mabel noticed a softness in Mrs. Lou that she hadn't seen in anyone else she had worked for.

"Did you ever see your family again?" Mabel asked.

"Oh, yes, I even went to see my mother at the old home place. That is how I met the 'love of my life.' I'll have to tell you that story some other time. We'd better get the food ready. These hungry boys and men will be here before we know it."

Mabel liked many things about the Hightower family. One was that Mr. Hightower always offered prayer before eating, just as Papa had always done. They also went to church and seemed to love God.

While Mabel was walking back to the Martin home that evening, she tried to remember a verse she had read in Deuteronomy. It said that if a person would love and obey God's commandments that God would bless their children forever. She remembered how carefully her papa had tried to obey God. *Thank You, Lord, for giving me a good place to work and a home with the Martins. I know You are blessing me because my papa and mama obeyed You. Help me always obey Your commandments that my children will also be blessed. Thank You that Mrs. Hightower is so very different from Mrs. McNally or Mrs. Snodgrass. Thank You again, dear Jesus.*

Questions for reflection:

1. What are some reasons why God blessed Mabel?
2. Do you think Mrs. Lou and Mabel understood each other?
3. How was Mrs. Lou's childhood different from Mabel's?
4. Did both Mrs. Lou and Mabel accept difficulties well?
5. What does God promise those who obey His commandments?

The Michael Hightower family, grandson of Mabel
and great grandson of Mrs. Lou Hightower.

*A soft answer turneth away wrath: but
grievous words stir up anger.*

Proverbs 15:1

STRANGE PROBLEMS

Every day was unusual at the Hightower home. The boys were as different as if they were from separate families.

Twelve-year-old James Ezra was calm, solemn, and meticulous about everything, especially about what he ate. However, sometimes when he got angry, he exploded like a volcano.

Cornelius was happy go lucky. He saw life as a package of fun to be enjoyed, at the moment. He wasn't troubled about the consequences of his actions. He knew that if he put a finger into Jim's dessert while passing it to him, Jim would not eat it. Then he and Aubrey would get to share it. This happened often. Mabel felt sorry for Jim.

One day Cornelius again put his thumb into Jim's pie as he passed it to him. "Do you still want the pie?" Cornelius asked.

"Yes," Jim replied. Jim took the pie, set it beside his plate and finished eating the food on his plate. Then he got up, took the pie in his hand, and walked slowly around the table. He stopped behind Cornelius and quickly shoved the pie, plate and all, into Cornelius' face, rubbing it up his nose. Then he put on his hat and disappeared out the door, leaving Cornelius coughing and sneezing. Mabel thought Cornelius got what he deserved.

Five-year-old Aubrey Earnest was the perfect child, according to his mother; but not everyone thought so. He was nick-named "Red" because of the deep red color of his hair. Mabel found the conflicts between Red and his older brothers to be a source of amusement.

Aubrey would often hold his breath when he did not get what he wanted. Mrs. Lou was sure he would die, and because she knew the pain of losing children in death, she would give him whatever he wanted. This made the other boys angry, for often they would have to give him something they wanted to keep. Alvin often murmured that he would break Aubrey of this terrible habit.

One evening, after a hard-day's work, Alvin slumped into a chair. An instant later Aubrey fell on the floor kicking and screaming. "What is he wanting?" Mrs. Lou asked. No one answered. Nor did they give up anything they had, so Aubrey tried his old trick. He stiffened out and did not breathe. Mrs. Lou bent over Aubrey, "Don't do that, Honey, you will die. What do you want? What is it Honey? Who has what he wants?" she demanded. No one offered to help. Aubrey kept on holding his breath. Mrs. Lou kept on trying to get him to breathe and to find out what he wanted.

Finally, Alvin jumped out of his chair and ordered, "Step back, and leave him alone. I'm going to cure him." Then snatching the bucket full of water that was sitting on a bench beside the door, he took two steps forward and poured the whole bucket of water over Aubrey.

"Alvin! Alvin!" Mrs. Lou yelled. "You're going to kill him just like Jim did the goslings." Aubrey immediately caught his breath and started spitting and sputtering. Mrs. Lou picked up Aubrey and ran into the other room. A stream of water trailed behind them. The other boys roared with laughter.

Mabel could hear Mrs. Lou comforting Aubrey. She shuddered while sweeping the water out the back door. Surely, Mrs. Lou would be angry. Mabel thought of Proverbs 15:1 *"A soft answer turns away wrath: but grievous words stir up anger."* Mabel was prepared to answer any question very softly; if no questions were asked, she would keep quiet, although she really wanted to know about the goslings.

Alvin must have felt guilty when Mabel had to stop preparing supper and sweep out the water. Taking the broom from her hand, he said, "I will clean up the water. I caused the mess."

Mabel busied herself again with the supper while Alvin was sweeping out the water. She stepped around water puddles, putting plates, silverware and glasses on the table. Mrs. Lou was still fussing with Aubrey in the bedroom. Finally, Aubrey got quiet for a while. When they came out Aubrey had on dry clothes.

Mrs. Lou came out in a sullen mood. Silence reigned. It was thick and eerie — so thick one might slice it with a knife. Even the boarders seemed unusually quiet that evening. After they had eaten, Mabel hurriedly cleaned the kitchen and left.

As she walked home, she wondered in what mood she would find Mrs. Lou the following day. Mabel was troubled about such quietness, until God reminded her of a verse in Isaiah which says, *The work of righteousness shall be peace; and the effect of righteousness quietness and assurance forever.* Mabel smiled to herself; she was seeing the Bible lived out by this family. Instead of everyone being upset and yelling at each other, they were quiet. Then another verse in Isaiah came to her mind. *In quietness and in confidence shall be your strength.* She said to herself, *then I too, shall be quiet.*

The following morning Mabel found Mrs. Lou in a pleasant talkative mood. It was wash day; so as they scrubbed clothes, each on her own scrub board, Mrs. Lou talked.

> *Last night after I calmed down, God caused me to think about my past life. As I thought about it, I realized how thankful I should be that I have Jim and the boys. Many years ago, we moved to Jackson County, Arkansas to a place called Big Bottom. Farming was wonderful, but there were masses of mosquitoes and malaria almost killed us.*

> *Jessie, my eleven-year-old half-sister, lived with us. I had three children: Artie, Alvin, and a little baby, Henry. Jessie was the only one well, so she took care of all five of us. Before we got well, my brother came to take her home.*

> *Jim thought he must get well before Jessie had to leave; so instead of taking just one spoon full of our prescribed medicine, he started drinking from the bottle. I shouted, 'You are going to kill yourself,' and I grabbed the bottle away from him. Sure enough, in about an hour, he fainted away.*

"Oh!" Mabel gasped. "Did he almost die?"

He sure did, but God had mercy on us. My brother ran to the neighbors for help. They handed him some whiskey and said, 'Pour this down em.' Jim aroused enough to swallow it. Whether it did any good, I don't know. But he lived.

When Jessie left, we had to take care of ourselves. Neither Jim nor I could be up for more than a few hours each morning. Then we'd have to go back to bed. The children were sick also and so puny because I couldn't care for them.

We left that mosquito-infested place as soon as we were able. We got as far as Sulphur Rock and ran out of money. We made a bargain to share crop for a farmer. I was sick the whole year we were there. I had big infected sores over my body. You know, what we call boils.

"Yes," Mabel said, "but why are they called boils? They don't boil."

"Maybe because they hurt as much as a burn from something boiling." They both laughed. "I think they do hurt that much. Anyway, I had a boil on my back, on my hip, in my hand, under my arm, and small ones in many other places over my body. Then in the fall, while Jim was gathering in the crop we had grown, our little Henry took sick. And Mabel, the sweet the sweet little thing, died a week later."

By now, Mrs. Lou was wiping tears and so choked up she couldn't speak. Mabel understood now why Mrs. Lou had been so frightened about Aubrey dying. "I'm so sorry," Mabel said.

"Oh, Mabel, death is awful! When you are among strangers it seems even worse. Although everyone was nice to us, there's nothing like your own family. I will be so glad when you find your papa."

"Oh, I will be too," Mabel said. She felt like crying with Mrs. Lou. Mabel also wanted to cry because of the fear that haunted her every day of not finding Papa. Even though when she prayed or read the Bible, she always felt more hopeful. But not wanting to miss any of Mrs. Lou's stories, she said, "And did you go back to your home place in Izard County?"

"No, we did not. We sold our share of the harvest and moved to another place in Jackson County. It was so painful to leave my little Henry in the cold ground in an unmarked grave. I knew I could never again go to his grave. I thought I just could not bear it. However, God was good and helped me to realize that Henry was not in the cold ground. Henry was a little angel in Heaven. Also, God helped me remember the many things for which to be happy. I had a good husband that loved and provided for me. I still had two of my children, Artie and Alvin, and I knew we could again be a happy family."

"Artie, is that a girl? I didn't know you had a girl. I'd like to meet her. Is she too far away to come visit?"

"Yes, she is too far away," is all that Mrs. Lou said.

"Excuse me, Mrs. Lou, for asking so many questions, but since you are sharing your life with me, may I ask one more? What were you saying yesterday about Jim and the goslings?"

"Oh, it wasn't a gosling, it was a ducky that little Jim killed. My James Ezra was a murderer from the beginning, but he never intended to kill anything. The first animal he killed was a puppy he loved dearly. While playing, he hit it on the head with a stick and it died. Our mama duck hatched out several ducklings. One day Jim thought one needed its face washed. When he begged me for a comb, I asked, 'Why do you want a comb?'

"He answered, 'Me washed ducky's face now me comb its hair.' Then I noticed him holding the duck by the throat. The little duckling was already limp so I knew it was also dead."

"I never thought James Ezra would do that."

"Oh, Mabel, you don't know my boys. They were very mischievous. But Alvin, he got into more trouble than all the others put together."

Questions for reflection:

1. Can you relate to doing things like Cornelius and Aubrey?
2. What are some things you do to get what you want?
3. Is it pleasing to God for children to fuss to get what they want?
4. Is it easy to answer softly when we are angry?
5. How did Mrs. Lou cope with discouragement?

Delight thyself also in the Lord; and he shall give thee the desires of thy heart.

Psalms 37:4

MY PAPA, MY PAPA

Mabel always tried to remember the Bible verses she read. Remembering them helped her to believe that God would protect her and supply what she needed and that she would find Papa. *'Trust in the Lord, and do good; so shalt thou dwell in the land, and verily thou shalt be fed. Delight thyself in the LORD; and he shall give thee the desires of thine heart,'* was the verse she had read last night before going to bed. *Lord,* she whispered as she was walking to work, *I believe You will soon give me the desire of my heart to be with Papa. I have trusted in You, and You have always supplied food for me, just as You promised. You also promised to give me the desire of my heart, which You know is to be with Papa again. These five years of being separated have been so long.*

As Mabel walked back and forth between her new job and the Martins, and whenever she went to church, she was always searching for her big bushy headed papa. *Surely he is somewhere among all these 90,000 people, Mabel thought. Mr. Martin and the street car driver had both said there were 90,000 people in Oklahoma City.*

Not many evenings after Mabel had prayed, Mr. Martin came in and said to his wife. "Let's take Mabel and go for a ride." As they rode through

Oklahoma City, Mabel was again looking for her Papa. She was so busy looking that she did not notice the police station that she had so feared. After they passed it, they went to the North side of town. From a wide street, Mr. Martin made a left turn, went a ways on a dirt street, then stopped in front of an apartment house.

"I'll be right back," Mr. Martin called, as he hurried around to the side door. Mabel saw him knocking; then heard him saying, "We're here." Immediately, a tall bushy headed man stepped out.

"My Papa, my Papa!" cried Mabel. She leaped from the car and ran like a rabbit running from a gray hound dog. She fell into Papa's open arms. "Papa, my Papa, is it really you?" she cried. After a moment, Mabel backed away and looked up into his big gentle face and patted his bushy red hair that was now streaked with gray.

"Oh Mabel, my baby Mabel," Papa sighed. He hugged her tightly again; and with his big hand, he laid her head on his chest. Then they both began sobbing. It was a long time before either moved. Mabel couldn't tear herself away from the strong safe arms of her papa, the one she had desired to see for so long—the one for whom she had taken many risks. She had left her only other family member and used all her savings hunting for him. She had prayed and hoped when she had no reason to hope. At last, she was not only seeing him, but touching him. She clung more tightly. It was too good to be true. Was it really true? She ran her hand up over his bushy red hair. It felt so good. Her heart was so full it felt like it might burst.

When Mabel could control her voice, she raised her head and looked into Papa's sad, blue eyes and said, *"Weeping does endure for a night, but joy comes in the morning.* Papa, that's the verse we used to say when Mama was so sick. Do you remember?"

"Oh, Mabel, I don't remember much, but I know all of God's Word is true."

"Yes, it is, and it says, *'I can do all things through Christ who strengthens me.'* And I did it, Papa. We did it."

She looked over at Officer Martin who was smiling. "We found you, Papa, like the verse says."

"Oh, Mabel, what courage you have. What joy you bring to me!"

Mrs. Martin had her arms around Mabel, trying to share her happiness. "Mabel has also brought joy to us," she said. "You have a jewel, not just a daughter. There is not another one like her in this world."

"I know, I know." Papa said, wiping his face, wet with tears. "I'm so sorry I had to leave her. And thanks for helping her and for all your efforts to find me."

"Pardon my leaping from the car. I guess my actions weren't proper for a seventeen-year-old," Mabel said to Mr. Martin.

"Never mind. Have happy days with Papa. We'll bring your things later. Right now, I'll go by and tell Mrs. Hightower the good news and that you won't be working for a few days."

"Oh! Thank you so much. I would love to have time to be with Papa." They shook hands with Papa, gave Mabel another hug, and drove away.

All evening Mabel sat beside Papa. They talked for hours about the many things that had happened in the five years they were apart.

Mabel told him about her little room at Mrs. McNally's where she prayed and read her Bible. She told him about the lovely big garden she helped tend and about the funny things the wild McNally children did. She told him about Mrs. Snodgrass' ridiculing her and how Old Joe had encouraged her to stay pure. She told how much Estella loved Wallace, and how they had taken her to the train station. She did not tell him about her disappointments or how afraid she was that first night in Oklahoma City.

"Oh, Mabel," he said, "I never thought when I left you that things would turn out like they did. The past years have been so hard for you. It broke my heart when Mr. Martin told me how he'd found you at night out on the street corner without a place to go." His chin quivered. He twisted his big hands together and said no more. He just sobbed, big heavy hard sobs, just as he had done that day when Mama died.

"Let's not talk about it," said Mabel. "God helped Mr. Martin find you, and that's all that matters. I'll write Estella tomorrow and tell her that we are together. Maybe she will come to see us."

After they had talked for a long time, Papa raised his head and said, "Yes, the most important thing is that we are together again. Maybe we had better get some rest now. The sun will soon be coming up."

"I'm not sleepy," Mabel said, as she traced the lines in his big hands. "I just want to look at you, to hear your voice, and feel your big strong arms. This seems like a dream. I'm afraid if I go to sleep, I will wake, and you will be gone. Then I'd have to start hunting all over again."

They both laughed.

"But you must rest, my child. All you have been through has been extremely hard for you. Let us pray and thank God for all His blessings."

"Oh, Lord Jesus," Papa prayed, "Thank You for keeping Mabel safe. Thank You with all my heart: for keeping her from following the evil ways of the world, for keeping her from smoking, drinking, and worse sins, and that You kept her pure while living at the hotel. You kept Your big hand over her and gave her a mind to be true to You. Please, dear God, give Albert, Estella, and Wallace a mind to do right. And we can never thank You enough for bringing us together again."

Far into the night, when Papa was laying on the floor snoring, Mabel had not gone to sleep. She was listening to Papa's heavy breathing. It was like music to her ears, yet she felt sorry that Papa had to labor so hard just to breath. She sat up in Papa's bed and looked around the little apartment. It was so meagerly furnished, a one-burner stove, a small table, two chairs, and the bed. She was thinking of ways to make it look like a home, a home with a woman in it. A little light was creeping into the only window when Mabel finally fell asleep.

Questions for reflection:

1. What was Mabel's promise from the Bible?
2. What helped Mabel to have faith?
3. Did God give Mabel the desire of her heart?
4. For how many years had Mabel not seen Papa?
5. What was the verse Papa and Estella had taught Mabel?

She looketh well to the ways of her household, and eateth not the bread of idleness.

Proverbs 31:27

MABEL AND PAPA MAKE A FAMILY

Although Mabel hadn't slept much during the night, she awoke early and found the flour, lard, baking powder, and salt. Then she made biscuits like she had seen Mrs. Lou do. The little one burner stove had no oven; so warming a large iron skillet, she melted a spoonful of lard in it and carefully placed the round biscuits in it. She put a lid on the skillet and turned the flame very, very low. While the bread was baking, she found eggs in a wire basket and a bit of ham Papa had left from his supper. She chopped the ham into small pieces and mixed it with three eggs.

"Mm mm, something smells good!" Papa said, as he stretched his long arms above his head and rolled over. "I'm surprised I slept so well on the floor. How did you sleep?"

"I slept well," Mabel answered. "However, often in the night I awoke to see if you were still here." They both laughed.

"Don't you worry; I won't leave again. You will probably leave me, when you find someone to marry."

"Oh, I know someone I'd like to marry. But I will have to wait until he asks me, and I don't think he has noticed me as yet. Anyway, I just want to take care of you now. I will soon have your breakfast ready."

"How wonderful! How did you know I was hungry for homemade biscuits?" Papa said when he saw them on the table.

"Don't all men like hot bread?" she questioned. "The men that eat at Mrs. Lou's sure do like her hot biscuits. Mrs. Lou is the lady I am working for. She is a Christian and seems to understand me better than the others I have worked for. She is really friendly, too, and tells me stories about her life."

"Say, Mabel, I am working now, so why don't you just quit working and rest for a while. I am sure you need a little time for reading and relaxing."

"Papa, that would be wonderful. I could do the housework and cook for you. Maybe you will get completely well."

Mabel helped Mrs. Hightower until she found another helper, then Mabel stayed home and cooked for Papa.

Every day a man came by with a wagon full of vegetables to sell. As his horse pulled the wagon down the street, the man called, "Vegetables, vegetables. Come buy vegetables." Mabel bought whatever he had. Papa especially loved fresh turnips, beets and spinach. Mabel loved to see Papa's happy face when she served him turnips and corn bread. Today the man had large beautiful carrots. Mabel bought several and some turnips. Papa's teeth were getting bad, so Mabel grated the carrots very fine so Papa could taste the delicious fresh uncooked carrots. Then she cooked turnips and corn bread.

Mabel kept her money in a cup above the stove. Early one morning, right after Papa went to work, Mabel heard, "Vegetables, vegetables." *He sure is coming early* Mabel thought, as she reached for her money. She hurried out the door. They lived in a rear apartment behind a house and beside another apartment house. She hurried between the two buildings out to the street, but the man and his wagon of vegetables were nowhere to be seen. Puzzled, Mabel started back to the apartment. As she walked, she heard laughter. "Vegetables, Vegetables," said the laughing voice, and it laughed again. There in the window of the next door apartment was a large Macaw parrot laughing at her.

"You ornery parrot," she said, and shook her finger at him. "You sounded just like the old vegetable man." The parrot laughed again.

Besides meeting the owner of the parrot, Mabel soon met others living in the apartment complex. The members of one family were spiritualists. They believed that spirits gave them power to do magical things. They could make a heavy flatiron dance, papers fly, and they could talk with people who were dead. Mabel thought it would be nice to talk with her mama or her brother, Little John.

The family lived in another building, but Mabel could look out of her window and into their apartment through their windows. She had seen a heavy pressing iron dance all over the table, and no one was touching it. One time she was pressing the wrinkles out of Papa's shirt, and when she sat her iron down, it moved around crazily. When it moved the second time, and she was not touching it, she looked over into their apartment and saw they were looking at her and laughing.

When she told Papa about it, he said:

Their power comes from the devil. Mabel, don't ever go to their meetings. Don't even let yourself be curious about it. I've talked to their leader. I've been to spiritualist meetings. They do not have the sweet spirit of Jesus.

You were too young to remember our experiences with the spiritualists in Missouri. They challenged your Uncle Henry and me, saying that our God was weaker than theirs. They said that we could not move a table if their spirit was on it.

We met with them to prove God was stronger. At first, we could easily lift the table because it was not a very heavy table. Although, after they did their rituals, neither Uncle Henry nor I could move it. Then I prayed, 'Oh, LORD, move this table for Jesus' sake.' Suddenly, we were able to get it off the floor. Uncle Henry lifted it several inches into the air and held it there a few seconds. When he turned it loose, the table popped back onto the floor as if a strong power was pushing it.

'Kelley is stronger than the devil,' someone shouted.

'Jesus is stronger than the devil,' I answered. Even they admitted the devil is the secret of their power. You don't want that spirit to get a hold on you, do you?

"No, Papa, I love Jesus and I hate the devil. The devil brings sickness and trouble. Jesus gives us comfort and peace. I'll always stay with Jesus. He is my best friend. He helped me while you were away. And He helped me find you."

"God bless you, Mabel."

Questions for reflection:

1. How did Mabel show she loved Papa?
2. What did Papa do that showed his love for Mabel?
3. What verse helped Mabel be a good home maker?
4. Why should Mabel not get curious about talking to the dead?
5. Did Papa want to protect Mabel from trouble?

The angel of the Lord encampeth round about them who fear him, and delivereth them.

Psalm 34:7

THE JOURNAL

Mabel went back to work when she realized that Mrs. Lou needed her help again. She also knew Papa was not doing well. She hoped if she was earning money that he would only need to work a few days each week. Besides that, Mabel enjoyed being in the Hightower's home. It was kind of like what she hoped her home would be when she got married. Mabel often wondered about their girl Artie. One day she said to Mrs. Lou, "We got a letter from Estella yesterday. Have you heard from Artie lately?"

"Oh, Mabel, I wasn't going to tell you about Artie. It's too painful to talk about."

"Why? Did Artie die, too?"

"Yes, my dear Artie is in heaven."

"Oh, I am so sorry. That is why you said she was too far away."

"Yes, but I can hardly talk about it, although it has been so many years ago." Mrs. Lou wiped a tear from her cheek. "However, while we are resting, I'll let you read in my journal what I wrote about Artie."

"Oh, really? I'd love to do that."

Mrs. Lou brought her journal from the bedroom and laid it on the table. She sat down and opened it to the page about Artie. Then she sat down in her rocking chair and laid her head back and closed her eyes.

Mabel began reading;

> *My dear little Artie died in the summer of 1897. Those bitter days of grief and sorrow never can be described. My first born, the joy of my life, the light of our home had flown. Our lives were so empty we could not comfort each other. Every leaf, every flower reminded me of her, until one night, I had a dream. I thought I passed a house with a porch in front of it. I found Artie sitting in a little rocker. When I went up to her, she said, 'Mama, do not grieve for me. I am happy. I am better off than you are. Why do you grieve for me? Do not grieve, Mama.' When I woke up the heaviness was gone. I was able to reason with myself and get relief.*

Mabel looked over at Mrs. Lou, who was wiping tears from her eyes. Mabel continued reading, but she read quietly to herself:

> *Then Alvin was all we had left, so of course we spoiled him; not that we did not control him, but all our attention went to him. I would hardly let him out of my sight except for sending him to school. Then the fall after Artie died, Alvin had brain fever. It looked for several days like we were going to have to give him up also. But through prayer and good nursing, plus a good doctor, he came through. It was five or six weeks before he could straighten his neck or hear when we talked to him.*

Mabel glanced over at Mrs. Lou and she seemed to be asleep. Mabel wanted to know everything about Alvin, so she kept reading. She often wondered why he was more Christian-like than his brothers.

> *Three of our old friends came from home and boarded with us several months. They were a great source of pleasure and help to us.*

> *When Alvin got well, we lived happily for about four more*
> *years with our one boy; and our whole life was centered*
> *in him. Of course we loved each other, but we both were*
> *sharing his life and happiness together. We kept him in*
> *school during the week and Sunday school on Sunday."*

Mabel said to herself, "Mmm— Alvin doesn't seem to be spoiled by all your love."

Instantly, Mrs. Lou was awake, "No, but he sure gave me some scares because he loved water. Seems like every time we went to a lake or river he would accidentally fall in. One of those times we were at a fish fry."

"Oh, yes, I saw that right here. May I read that too?" questioned Mabel. She read aloud.

> *Everyone took food. We spread our tablecloths on the grass*
> *and fried fish and had a lovely time, except Alvin came*
> *along with another one of his tricks. He was walking near*
> *the river holding to the bushes, and, as could be expected,*
> *a twig broke and down came Alvin into the river, head over*
> *heels. He was wet and had no dry clothes to put on, so we*
> *wrapped him up and hung his clothes in the sunshine to dry.*
> *The next time we went to a country picnic on the fourth of*
> *July it rained and we all got wet, so Alvin could laugh at us.*

"Oh, Mrs. Lou, your journal is so interesting. God's angels were always watching over you."

"Oh yes, the Lord has faithfully watched over us. And He will watch over you, Mabel, wherever you live or wherever you are working; God will send His angel to care for you."

"Yes, I know. He has always cared for me even when I was alone and afraid."

"God is good to everyone; but tomorrow camp meeting starts, and I have a lot to do to get ready for that. We'll have to get back to work now."

Days and weeks passed, and Mrs. Lou never seemed to have time to talk; so Mabel was still wondering why Alvin gave her so much trouble and if Mrs. Lou would ever tell how she and Mr. Hightower met.

Summer was about over and Papa would soon be going back to work. Mabel noticed that he was having lots of trouble breathing. He had been wheezing for many weeks now. Mabel hoped he wouldn't have to leave her again to go looking for a place where he could breathe easier. Then she thought of a plan.

After they ate supper and she cleaned up the kitchen, she moved her chair close to his and took his big hand in hers. "Papa," she said, "I went back to work for Mrs. Hightower because I think you need to stop working and rest. I've been noticing how difficult it is for you to breathe."

"I don't believe rest is the answer. This Oklahoma wind and dust is getting me down."

"So you think another climate might be better for you? I'd be willing to go with you wherever."

"Mabel, it's like you read my thoughts. I haven't mentioned it to you, because I feared it would be too hard on you to again stay alone or to move to another place and have to find another job. You seem to be happy working for Mrs. Hightower."

"Yes, Papa, I am happy with them, as long as I can see you each evening. Papa you are more important to me than anything. Now where do you think would be a good place for us to live?"

"I don't know, but I've a yearning to go back to Missouri. I was able to work every day when we lived there; also, we have family there."

"Family? Who?" Mabel asked.

"Your cousins, Loren, Henry, and Uncle John's children."

"I have been thinking of Estella and Albert. I do wonder how Estella is feeling. According to her last letter, she wasn't able to take care of Harold and Geraldine. Wallace's mother was taking care of her children. Don't you think she may have the same sickness that Mama had?"

"Yes, I do. We may not have Estella with us much longer."

"Oh, how I wish I could go and see her."

"It would be nice, but how could we?"

"I know we can't. It took me six months to save enough for the ticket when I came here."

"And she may not last that long," Papa said, and he began twisting his hands. Mabel saw a tear slip down his cheek.

"Don't worry, Papa," she said. "God will be with her as He has been with us. Remember, God never leaves nor forsakes His children; and there isn't any way we can help her. She said that Wallace's mother is taking care of her and the children. Maybe we should go on to Missouri where you could feel better—and maybe—just maybe maybe we will learn something about Albert. Perhaps someone of the family has heard from him."

"Mabel, you are so willing."

"Papa, it's because I have learned to trust in God, wherever we are. God is always watching over us. His angels are camping around us all the time to protect us."

"That is true; we can move and be safe from harm."

"Then let's start saving whatever we can spare so if you do get worse, we will have money to make the move."

"Okay," Papa answered.

Every day when Mabel went to work she hoped Mrs. Lou would tell her more about the Hightower family before she had to leave. She was still wondering why Alvin caused Mrs. Lou so much trouble and how Mrs. Lou had met Mr. Hightower. Even so, they were very busy with spring house cleaning and there was little time to talk. Mabel also wanted to tell Mrs. Lou that she might not be working much longer.

After a few weeks passed and they had not talked much, Mabel told Mrs. Lou of their plan to move if Papa's health worsened.

"The Lord will be with you," Mrs. Lou told Mabel. "I know it is kind of hard to move, for we have moved a lot. In 1910 we moved to Wise Town, Arkansas; that is where Jim had grown up. He raised his siblings on his dad's farm there. When Jim was 16, his father, Noel Watkins Hightower, was splitting logs to build a new log cabin and accidentally hit his leg. It was a bad cut. He lost a lot of blood, and he died shortly afterward. Jim always wanted to go back there, so we moved there and bought a sawmill and gristmill."

"Alvin was 19 then, and one day he was oiling the machinery of the mill and his glove caught in the machine, causing it to twist his arm. His arm broke in two places. It took two months to heal. Shortly after that, Jim's sister came to live with us. She lived only a few days and died. We buried her beside Jim's dad and brother. Then Jim, Ezra, and I took sick. Because of so much trouble, we left that place after two years and came back here to Oklahoma.

"We lived here a short while and moved back again to Arkansas. We lived there about five years and came again to Oklahoma City."

"So you must have just returned when I met you?"

"Yes, we had just moved in here."

"You have moved a lot; but you have had very interesting experiences," Mabel said, hoping it might inspire Mrs. Lou to talk. And it did.

"Yes, Alvin was forever getting hurt," she said very thoughtfully. "It wasn't that he was a bad boy. I wonder if God was testing my faith, because after I lost both Henry and Artie, I almost worshipped Alvin."

Questions for reflection:

1. Why was Mabel working again for Mrs. Lou?
2. How did God comfort Mrs. Lou when her little girl died?
3. How do you think Mabel felt about not seeing Estella again?
4. What has God promised to those who fear him?
5. Does God always watch over his children?

Mabel in the Item Bakery in Oklahoma City
while she was working there.

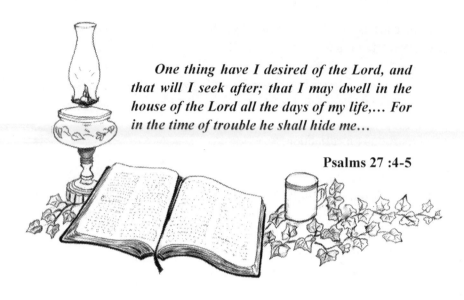

One thing have I desired of the Lord, and that will I seek after; that I may dwell in the house of the Lord all the days of my life,... For in the time of trouble he shall hide me...

Psalms 27 :4-5

A BETTER JOB FOR MABEL

The trees were turning gold and brown and days were getting cooler. Mabel knew Papa might not be able to go out on some cold snowy winter days. She must find a job where she could earn more money so she could help with winter expenses. Papa and she both needed new winter coats. Heating bills were always high in the winter. In icy cold weather when they could not walk safely, a taxi would have to be paid. She remembered a verse in Proverbs that says people should learn from the ants, for the ants stock extra food to use in the winter. She laughed. "I guess I'm like an ant, I'm preparing for winter."

Her thoughts wandered back to her and Papa's conversation a few months ago. They had decided to move back to Missouri in hopes that Papa would feel better there. However, God had blessed Papa, and he was working every day. Mabel was again staying home.

Mabel loved being a housekeeper; she loved cooking, especially baking bread. She loved to finger the flour and the butter, and it always amazed her how a tiny bit of yeast could make dough grow and grow until it was double or triple its original size.

The thing she liked most about home was getting to read. Today she was reading the book she loved best, the Bible. She read Psalms. 21:2 *Thou hast given him his heart's desire, and has not withholden the request of his lips.*

Mabel bowed her head and said, *Yes, God has given me the desire of my heart to be with Papa and to have a good place to work. Although I worked hard, Mrs. Hightower shared her life's story, making me feel as if she really cared about me.*

Getting to go to church with Papa was also a desire of Mabel's heart. Mabel had gone to church alone, even when Mrs. Snodgrass made fun of her for doing so. Now she was going with Papa and had many church friends. Even the Hightower family was again attending the same church she attended. The day they came, Mabel was leading the singing. She heard that Alvin said that he loved her singing. She also loved to hear Alvin and his brothers sing. Even the pastor said, "Those boys can make more music than the whole congregation." Mabel thought so, too, yet hearing them sing wasn't nearly as great as listening to Papa's strong tenor voice.

Mabel picked up her Bible again and began reading in Psalms 27:4. *One thing have I desired of the Lord, that will I seek after; that I may dwell in the house of the Lord all the days of my life, to behold the beauty of the Lord, and to inquire in his temple. For in the time of trouble he shall hide me in his pavilion: in the secret of his tabernacle shall he hide me; he shall set me up on a rock.* She again covered her face with her hands and said, *Thank You God for that promise. Thank You for keeping me from evil desires when Mrs. Snodgrass tempted me to do wrong. My heart seeks after You. I want to know You better every day. You are more precious to me than Papa. You have been beside me all the while that Papa wasn't. Thank you Jesus. You are setting me up on a rock, and that rock is Christ Jesus.*

Since the apartment was already clean, Mabel went out looking for work. "I will soon be twenty, so now I should be able to find a job in a business," she said to herself as she walked out the door of their apartment on east 10th Street. She was soon close to downtown. She gazed at the many tall hotel buildings and shivered at the thought of washing sheets and mopping floors in another hotel. There were department stores. *Maybe I could be a clerk in one of those*, she said to herself. *Working in a restaurant would be fine if I didn't have to wash dishes. I hate washing dishes.* Just then, Mabel smelled the aroma of freshly baked bread. *That is what I want to do. I want to work in a bakery and learn to make bread.* She followed her nose like a dog after a bone. There it was, the Item Bakery on the corner of Washington and Compress.

When Papa came home, Mabel met him at the door and threw her arms around him. "Papa, I've great news! I have a job at the Item Bakery. Isn't that wonderful? I can learn how to bake bread."

"Mabel, my baby, I hope you won't work too hard. It sure will be hot in the summer working near hot ovens."

"Maybe so, but how warm and cozy it will be when snow is on the ground. Oh, Papa, the building is so big. It is five stories high."

"Just let me sit down and then tell me all about it." He said as he pulled away and slumped into the nearest chair.

"Look, I've a pamphlet that tells all about it. I'll read it to you." Mabel began reading:

> *This building, five stories high, plus a basement, is built of reinforced concrete and brick and is the largest of all Item Biscuit plants. It employs 150 people and is expanding. Now that John Item has moved to the city it may possibly employ 300 persons. The furnaces and ovens are on the top floor. Icing is on the 4th, packing on the 3rd, and shipping on the 1st. Many of the items will be packed in tin boxes and sold by traveling salesmen as well as in retail stores.'*

"Oh, Papa, I'm so happy. It's just what I wanted."

"Remember God said, 'Delight thyself in the Lord; and he shall give thee the desires of thine heart.' So that is what He did."

"Oh, Papa, that is so true."

Monday morning Mabel caught the streetcar and rode it down the hill to the bakery. When she got off, people were everywhere. It reminded her of her first day of school in Mangum. However, today she didn't feel lonely or afraid. God had given her this job. She knew He was with her.

A woman met her at the door and placed a hat on Mabel's head. "This must be worn at all times while inside. It is to keep stray hairs out of the boxes of crackers and cookies."

Questions for reflection:

1. Why did Mabel like staying at home?
2. What did Mabel like best to do at home?
3. What was Mabel's favorite book?

4. What had Mabel wanted that God had given to her?
5. Why did Mabel want to work in a bakery?

Estella M. Kelley Adair 1895-1925

...Whither thou goest, I will go; and where thou lodgest, I will lodge: thy people shall be my people and thy God my God."

Ruth 1:16

SAD NEWS FROM MANGUM

Mabel had been noticing for some time that Papa's breathing was again getting difficult. He was missing many days of work and could hardly carry on a conversation without wheezing. One day he brought home a new trunk. "Mabel," he said in a sorrowful tone "I—I—I— know you are happy at the bakery and have many friends here in Oklahoma City. I hate to uproot you again, but I think we had better go ahead and move back to Missouri. You would have some family if my health gets worse."

"Oh, Papa, I hope nothing will happen to you. However, I know you have been suffering a long time. You have tried hard to stay well for my sake. You and I both will probably feel better being around family. We have no family here. Estella is so far away. I think Wallace and his mother are taking good care of her and little Geraldine and Harold."

Papa laid his head in his hands. "Don't feel bad, Papa," Mabel said. "Moving will be the best. I'll tell them at the bakery that I'm leaving. Then I will get our trunk packed as soon as possible. God will take care of us. Remember your song, 'Jesus Will Save and Keep'? Jesus will keep us wherever we go."

Papa looked up. Mabel noticed the tired stressful wrinkles on his forehead. "Mabel, before we leave, why don't you take off a few days and go visit with your friends?"

"I'd love to, especially Mrs. Lou. Maybe I could find out how she met Mr. Hightower."

A few days before leaving, Mabel went to visit Mrs. Lou. "I've come to say goodbye," Mabel said. "Papa is badly sick again, so we're going to Neosho, Missouri to be near family."

"I'm so sorry. I do hope he does better in a different climate."

Mabel asked about each boy. Then she said, "Thank you for sharing your life's story with me."

"You are quite welcome, but you never heard how I met Jim."

"No, I didn't. I would love to know."

"Sit down and I will tell you:

When I was sixteen, my mother became very ill. My brother came and took me home to see her. You see, I lived with old Dr. Morris. We only lived 50 miles apart, but it took two days on horseback to go the distance. Mother's folks and another family carried water from the same spring. One night my brother James said, 'Lou, I want you to go with me to the spring. I want you to see two white-headed young men' (one was Jim). So I went.

In a few days, Jim came to Mother's house and asked about me. I already had my love, Willie Durent. But Mama insisted that I be nice to Jim, so I was polite to him. When the time came to start home, lo and behold, Jim Hightower came with his wagon to drive us to Dr. Morris' place. Mama and my brother came along. A few days later, here came a letter from Jim. We wrote only friendly letters that winter. Toward the last of February, my brother came again for me. As soon as I got to Mother's house, Jim Hightower was there; and he came to see me almost every day while I was visiting Mother.

I will never forget the morning that he came to tell me 'good-bye.' As we were standing on Mother's porch talking,

> *he said, 'Lou, I have to move out to the farm to take care*
> *of things. Won't you go with me? I can't live without you.'*
>
> *I had got to the place I could not withstand his pleadings,*
> *so I said. 'Yes, I will go with you.'*
>
> *He said, 'Will you marry me next Sunday?'*
>
> *I said, 'You don't give me much time to get ready.'*
>
> *'You don't need much time. I need you. What about next*
> *Sunday?'*
>
> *There I lost myself and said, 'Yes,' again. And I gained*
> *my life's happiness. We got married the following Sunday,*
> *March 10, 1889. (I was 17, Jim was 28)*

"Mabel, those are sweet memories. God has been so good to my family and me."

"Thank you for sharing with me," Mabel said. "It makes me feel that I am important to you. Nevertheless, I must be going. I'll say good-bye to Elsie Egermeier, Maud Hornbeck, and Ira Stover at church Sunday, and also I hope to see Mrs. Hunter and Mrs. Britten.

When Mabel entered the apartment, Papa was lying on his bed asleep. She was careful not to awake him. She sat down, and her thoughts went back to the time she was working for Mrs. Hunter.

One day Mabel and Mrs. Hunter went shopping. It was supposed to be a day of fun; however, to begin with, the day was far to hot to go shopping—especially for black shoes. A pair of sandals or white shoes would have been better. Mrs. Hunter thought if she wore plain black dresses and plain black shoes she would look like a saint. Mabel associated saints with angels and wondered how an angel dressed in black and wearing black shoes would look. Anyway, she was just the servant girl, although Mrs. Hunter tried to treat her like a friend and sister in the church.

Every store had an abundances of black shoes, however not one pleased Mrs. Hunter. One had a gold buckle, another had a red flower, and the heel was a bit too high on others. Mabel shielded her head from the blazing sun as they walked from shop to shop or while waiting for the streetcars. Mrs.

Hunter shaded her body with a silk umbrella. They climbed on and off, first one streetcar after another, all day long. *That disgusting day burned its way into my memory,* Mabel said to herself. *I think it shall be there forever.*

A heavy knock at the door caused Mabel to jump to her feet. She opened the door. "A telegram for Mr. Simon Pleasant Andrew Kelley," said a boy. "Does he live here?"

"Yes, he does," Mabel, answered.

The boy handed Mabel an envelope edged in black. Mabel's hand trembled as she reached for the telegram. She knew by the black edging, that someone had died.

"Papa, Papa," she said gently. "Wake up you have a telegram. It might be from Wallace."

Papa took the telegram. His hands were also trembling as he opened it. "Wallace," he said, and his chest started heaving and his breath came hard. When he got control enough to speak he said, "Here, Mabel, I can't read it."

Mabel was already wiping tears. She took the telegram, cleared her throat, and read: *Dear Estella left this morning,* she stopped. Her chin quivered. She looked over at Papa, who was looking up at the ceiling. He had that faraway look on his face that he had had when Mother Mary died. Mabel continued reading, *"Harold and Geraldine okay. Mother taking good care of them. Wallace"* Mabel paused again and then added, "Poor Harold and Geraldine, without a mother. How will they make it?" She sat down in a chair beside the table and laid her head on the table.

"Another one in heaven," Papa said. "Yes, another one. Lord help us to make it through this dark world that we might be with our folks again." He bowed his head and began sobbing again. But it was too much for him. He started coughing, then wheezing and having an asthma attack.

Mabel hurried to his chair, and put her hand on his shoulder, then she closed her eyes in prayer. "Don't cry Papa; it will make you sick. Estella is okay. She won't suffer any more. You know how much Mama suffered. You don't want Estella to suffer like that."

Papa was still gasping for breath, but he shook his head, "No."

When Mabel opened her eyes, she saw Estella's picture sitting on the table. "Look, Papa, how beautiful Estella is; won't she make a beautiful angel?"

Papa shook his head again.

Beside the picture was the song Papa had written. "Oh, Papa here is your song. I'll read it to you. Maybe it will encourage you. You know Jesus is the same today as when you wrote this."

Mabel read:

> "Jesus Saves and keeps
> Jesus is the truth and way
> He is just the same today,
> As when he calmed the raging sea,
> He can do the same for thee.
>
> Chorus
> Jesus saves from sin today,
> Keeps us in the narrow way,
> Whosoever will obey,
> He will keep him every day.
>
> How I love to serve the Lord,
> For it makes us one accord.
> Every one that's born again
> Christ is dwelling there within.
>
> If you will be born again
> You must let Christ reign within,
> Reign and rule over every part,
> For you must from sin depart.
>
> Jesus has subdued the foe,
> And we conquer as we go,
> In the name of Jesus Christ
> We are reigning in this life.
> By Simon Pleasant Andrew Kelley, my dear papa."

Questions for reflection:

1. Why did Papa believe they should move?
2. What did Mabel do before moving away?
3. Where do Christian people go when they die?
4. Why did Papa want to go to heaven?
5. What did Mabel do to comfort Papa?

Mabel's new Friend, Ella Mae Hughes (Huskey)

A man that hath friends, must show himself friendly...

Proverbs 18:24

MABEL FINDS A NEW FRIEND

Mabel stood in the Webb City post office reading a letter from Wallace. She was wiping tears from her face when a crippled girl came in. Mabel looked down at her feet. One leg was shorter than the other one. Underneath the shoe that she wore on the short leg, a metal brace extended below her shoe about three inches. Her adorable smile caused Mabel to want to meet her at once. Yet, before Mabel could decide what to say, the girl spoke. "I am Ella Mae Hughes," she said cheerfully. "You look sad. Did you get bad news in your letter?"

"It —It's— from my brother-in-law telling of my sister's sickness and death. She's my only sister. I have only one brother and we haven't been able to locate him since he left us in Mangum, OK."

"I'm so sorry. You must feel lonely. Aren't you new in town? I haven't seen you before."

"My name is Mabel Kelley. My papa and I moved here from Oklahoma. We wanted to live around Neosho or Pineville where our family lives, but there were no jobs to be found."

"Did your papa come here to find work in the lead and zinc mines?"

"No, my papa has asthma. We came here hoping the climate will help him to recover."

"And your mother?"

"She died in Neosho when I was seven years old."

"Oh, that is so sad."

"I am a baker. I found a job at the Nabisco bakery in Joplin."

"That would be an interesting job. So you ride the Webb City Northern to work every day."

"Yes, I ride the street car. But I see there is a shirt factory and a leather factory here. I might have found work at one of those. I think they would be good places to work."

"We have lots of new factories here. There is a box factory, a casket factory, and several other factories. During the war the mines around here were running day and night, and many people moved here. They say the mines earned 18 million dollars in 1914. There are about 700 mines in this area. By 1920 there were 15,000 people living here. Many of these were working in the mines. Then after the war ended, the mining business slowed way down. That is when our mayor started asking industries to come in so all those miners would still have jobs."

"Looks like his plan worked."

"Well, yes it did, and that year Webb City showed an increase in industry more than any city in the whole United States. And now Miss–– what did you say your name was?"

"I am Mabel Kelley."

"Oh, yes, Miss Mabel, now you know a little about the city where you are living." Both girls laughed. "I think I was a little excited about introducing you to my home town. I hope you like it as well as I do. Do you live nearby?

"We live on South Walker."

"That's near where I live. We live at 512 South Devon St. We might as well walk toward home together if you are going home now." As the girls walked slowly along on the brick sidewalk, Ella Mae continued talking. "My family attends the Church of God. It's a block up the street from our home. Are you a Christian?"

"Yes, I am. My mother told us to obey God and we would see her in heaven. So every day I ask God to help me obey Him."

"I am so sorry your mother died. Life must be painful without a mother."

"It has been discouraging at times, and I've had disappointments. Even so, verses from the Bible have kept me encouraged."

"I like Bible verses, also. My dad reads a Psalm and prays with our family every evening. We call it family worship," Ella Mae said, as she faced Mabel; "I must turn here. I'd love for you to start coming to church with me."

"I'd be happy to, if Papa does not mind staying home alone. I attended a Church of God in Oklahoma City. There were many churches in that city and several were named Church of God."

"We'd be happy to have your papa, too."

"My papa is really particular about where he goes to church. There was only one church that he would attend in Oklahoma City, and I think he had tried almost all of them. He says most churches aren't teaching what Jesus taught."

"We have lots of churches here also, maybe eighteen or twenty. I think your Papa will like what's being taught in the church where I go," she added with a sparkle in her eye. "I'll be by to get you early Sunday morning. Okay? And it's been nice meeting you."

"I'll be ready if Papa thinks it's all right. Good-bye!"

When Mabel got back to the apartment, she told Papa about her new friend, Ella Mae.

"A man that hath friends, must show himself friendly..." Papa quoted the Bible verse found in Proverbs.

"I always try to be friendly," she answered.

Before many weeks, Mabel was going to the church every chance she got, and Ella Mae was visiting their home regularly. Finally, when Papa was feeling better, he too went with her.

On the way home, Papa said, "You know I think maybe that church is a good one."

"I told you," Mabel said.

"I notice the girls are dressed modestly like the Bible says they should, and they were very friendly to you. What did you say their names are?"

"Ersa Carrick and Glenna Lawson are the two that hung around longer."

"And the young man that seemed so friendly?"

"He is Amos Porter, and, Papa, he plays the mandolin and sings beautifully like the Hightower boys."

"God has certainly been good to us," Papa said, and he began singing "Jesus Has Been so Good to Me."

"How amazing that you can walk and have breath to sing!" Mabel exclaimed.

Ella Mae's father, Mr. Willie Hughes, also began visiting them. He would bring a sack of flour, fresh or canned fruit or vegetables, or something else they needed. Sometimes Ella Mae's mother sent food ready to eat. This gave Mabel a chance to rest or catch up on other housework. Papa and Brother Hughes, as everyone called him, discussed the scriptures, and to Mabel's surprise, they agreed on many.

Ella Mae brought books to share with Mabel. However, after working nine hours a day at the bakery, then cooking, cleaning, and washing clothes at home, Mabel had very little time left for reading; however, she tried to read the Bible every day, even though sometimes she fell asleep doing so. Ella Mae wanted to help Mabel; but she could not help with the work because of her legs, so she read Mabel inspiring stories about missionaries and preachers while Mabel was scrubbing clothes or preparing food.

One day when Ella Mae was reading to Mabel the book of *Cripple Tom*, Mabel asked Ella Mae why she was crippled. Just when Ella Mae began explaining the accident that left her crippled, Papa took a coughing spell. Mabel ran to help him. She brought a glass of cold water and fanned him until her arms were tired. Ella Mae just looked on with scared eyes.

After Papa was comfortable, Ella Mae whispered to Mabel, "I thought your papa was going to die."

"This is very common," Mabel said. "Two or three times in the night, I'm helping him through one of these attacks."

Besides suffering with asthma, Papa's heart was failing, and he also had poor digestion. Mabel had to cook the food until it was very tender and then mash it before he could eat.

Mr. Hughes was a man of inventions, always thinking of new and better ways of doing things. If there wasn't a machine to make a job easier, he would make one. After Ella Mae told her father that Mr. Kelley couldn't eat solid food, he went looking for a food grinder.

The day he gave Papa the food grinder, Papa exclaimed, "You are like the Bible character, Dorcas, who spent her life helping others."

Mr. Hughes just laughed. Mabel washed the food grinder, and Mr. Hughes showed her how to use it. Then he and Ella Mae left.

Mabel placed a piece of cooked meat into the food grinder, turned the handle around and around, and out came the meat, finely ground. Mabel placed the meat on a plate, added some mashed potatoes, gravy, and finely chopped cabbage. While Papa was eating, she washed the grinder and ground a fresh apple. "This is the best meal I've eaten in a long, long time," Papa said.

While Mabel was eating, she asked, "Papa, do you think God brought Dorcas back to life because of all the good works she did or because the people needed her?"

"The Bible does not say. Perhaps it was because the widows and the poor needed her."

They were both silent for a while, then Mabel asked, "If Ella Mae should die, do you think God would give her life again?"

"Why do you ask?" questioned Papa.

"Because she is as helpful as Dorcas, and—and I—I— I need her just as they needed Dorcas."

Questions for reflection:

1. What can you tell about the city where you live?
2. In what ways did Ella Mae show a Christlike spirit?
3. How many people have you invited to come to church?
4. To what Bible character did Mabel liken Ella Mae?
5. What kind of man was Ella Mae's father?

Ella Mae's home at 512 S. Devon St., Webb City, Missouri.

...It is more blessed to give than to receive.

Acts 20:35

PAPA'S SURPRISE

Mabel had three work dresses and a nice one for Sunday. She had seen some pretty calico in the dry goods store uptown that she had hoped to buy before Easter. Each of her friends had gotten a new summer dress for Easter. Now it was almost June and she was still wearing her old wintery-looking dress. She picked up the little box containing her savings and counted every cent. "Almost enough," she said hopefully. "I should have enough left over from my next pay check to buy that material."

With the wages Mabel earned at the Nabisco bakery in Joplin, she bought food, paid the apartment rent and utilities, and bought a few other things they needed. Only a little was left for clothing. Papa was such a big man that his pants and shoes had to be special made, which made them very expensive. Mabel tried to save a little back from each pay check for clothing. It took a long time to save enough to buy Papa's clothing. However, now that Mr. Hughes was helping them, Mabel had saved almost enough to buy material to make herself a new dress.

All week Mabel dreamed about the new dress. Every evening as she passed the store, she looked through the window at the pretty material. Thursday evening she decided which one she would buy and planned how she'd have it made. "I'll take it over to the dressmaker as soon as I get it," she said to herself. "By the time the dressmaker has it finished, I'll have the money to pay for her labor."

As she walked on down the sidewalk, she noticed a SALE sign in the men's clothing store. She stopped to look. "How I wish I could buy Papa a shirt for Father's Day. I think this store would have one large enough for him," she said to herself. Then she noticed the sale price. *Wow! How could I ever save that much money?* she mumbled as she walked on toward home.

When payday came, Mabel hurried home and put on her very best dress, took out her savings, and added a little from her week's wages. There was enough for the material! "I'll be back soon and make your supper," she told Papa. "I must get into the dry goods store before it shuts for the night."

On the way to the store she met Ella Mae. "How nice to see yo*u!*" exclaimed Mabel. "I'm going now to buy material for a new dress. Do you know a good dressmaker, one who sews well but doesn't charge a lot for her work?"

"Mrs. Short, who lives on Webb Street, does very good work for a reasonable price," Ella Mae answered.

"Thank you so very much. I must hurry on before the store closes."

"Can you take just one minute to see what I have bought my papa for Father's Day?" asked Ella Mae as she opened her package.

"What a beautiful shirt," exclaimed Mabel. "A gift like that should make any papa happy!"

"I think my papa will like it. Well, I'll see you later. Good-bye." Mabel's head dropped lower and lower as she walked along. Her heart ached. All she could think about was Papa's old faded shirts, so threadbare. She dared not scrub them hard lest they tear into threads. When she finally raised her head, she was in front of the men's clothing store again. She saw a shirt like the one Ella Mae showed her. Behind it she noticed a sign "Give a shirt for Father's Day."

She walked on muttering to herself, *Don't I wish I could! Oh how I wish Albert would come back and live with us; he and I together could share living expenses and then we could buy Papa the clothes he needs. We could become a happy family together. God, won't You send Albert back to us? He's been gone so long.*

At the dry goods store, the clerk showed Mabel several pieces of material that she hadn't seen before. How beautiful they were! Now Mabel couldn't decide which she wanted. Besides, she was thinking about Father's Day.

With several different pieces in her hand, she walked over to a long mirror, which hung on the South wall. She draped one piece at a time over her shoulder, pretending to be seeing which looked best on her. She was really deciding if they would be suitable for a shirt.

Back at the material counter, she asked, "Do you have an inexpensive piece suitable for a man's shirt?" The clerk showed her several. "I will take this blue one. It will look good on my papa because his eyes are blue," Mabel said. She walked out of the store with a light, happy heart.

Denying herself for someone else always made her feel great. She took the material right over to Mrs. Short, the dressmaker, in hopes the shirt would be ready for Father's Day. Then she hurried home to prepare supper. She had worked hard all day, had walked home, back to town, and over to the dressmaker's. *It has been a long day, but I feel wonderful! S*he thought.

Father's Day, Mabel woke early and prepared a special breakfast for Papa. Then she brought out his new shirt. "Mabel, you shouldn't have done this for me." Papa said, "I know you did without something you needed. Oh, Mabel, there isn't a daughter like you anywhere on this earth."

"Papa, I wanted you to have it for Father's Day; besides, you really needed it."

While they were sitting in church, Mabel looked over at Ella Mae sitting beside Mr. Hughes. Mabel smiled. She thought Papa looked every bit as nice in his new blue shirt as Mr. Hughes did in the one that Ella Mae had bought for him.

Questions for reflection:

1. What verse did Mabel obey?
2. Why were Papa's clothes so expensive?
3. For what was Mabel saving some money?
4. Why did Mabel not buy her dress material?
5. Did giving to others make Mabel happy?

Mabel went to church meetings in Neosho whenever she had time. These are friends at a tent camp meeting in Neosho, Missouri, 1926. Ella Mae Hughes is second from the left.

She stretcheth out her hands to the poor;
yea, she reacheth forth her hands to the needy.

Proverbs 31:20

LOVE IN ACTION

Mabel shut off the vacuum cleaner and looked out the window at the beautiful Corpus Christi Bay. Sails on the boats seemed to be waving goodbye as they floated out of the bay and into the Gulf of Mexico. Mabel wondered where the people were going and what they would see. The white seagulls soaring overhead caused her to notice the great expanse of blue sky. *Where does space end?* she questioned. *Is heaven on the other side of it? Then how far is heaven? Maybe light years away? How awesome! And someday I'll get to go there.*

In her mind, Mabel could see Estella flying through space and meeting her mother, Mother Mary and Little John as they welcomed her into Heaven. How Mabel longed to see them, too. *What are they doing just now? I really want to know,* she said to herself. *I will never know that, but one thing I do know is that I will see them again.*

The doctor in Joplin had told Papa he should move to the southern coast, where the climate was warm, and the air was clean and fresh. But Papa thought it best to go back to Oklahoma City where they could be among people they knew and Mabel could possibly find work more easily. Mabel did find a job at the Wilson Meat Packing House in Oklahoma City, where the Hightower boys were working. However, Papa grew worse in windy, dusty Oklahoma. So as soon as they gathered enough money, they moved on to Corpus Christi, Texas. There the average January temperature is 57 degrees, and the air is always fresh. Living in Corpus Christi was like having spring all year: no scorching heat, no icy wind, no snow. Mabel loved it.

Mabel had found a good job cleaning in a hotel. Those years working with Mrs. Snodgrass were being a blessing. She could clean very well.

Mabel glanced at the clock on the hotel wall. It was time for her mid-morning break, so she sat down on a chair in the room she was cleaning and took her Testament from her pocket. She opened it and read again what she had read early that morning before coming to work.

I would not have you to be ignorant, brethren, concerning them which are asleep (or dead), that ye sorrow not, even as others which have no hope. For if we believe that Jesus died and rose again, even so them also which sleep in Jesus will God bring with him....Then we which are alive and remain shall be caught up together with them in the clouds, to meet the Lord in the air: and so shall we ever be with the Lord. I Thessalonians 4:13, 14, 17

Although only Papa and her were left, Mabel knew she would again be together with her family. Either she would go to meet them in Heaven or they would come back again with Jesus when He comes to get all His children.

When break time was over, Mabel cleaned the bathroom, emptied the wastepaper baskets, and mopped the floor. The beautiful room was clean. She must hurry; she had six more rooms to clean and the day was passing quickly.

Many wealthy people came to Corpus Christi because of the wonderful climate. As Mabel worked among the rich who stayed in the hotel, she learned that the rich, as well as the poor, have problems. Mrs. Kirkpatrick, a very wealthy woman, was taking treatments and hoping to be well again. She would have gladly given all her money to be healthy. Papa and this wealthy woman had come to Corpus Christi for the same reason. Mabel learned that money can't buy the most valuable things in life. Mabel sang as she went about her work and tried in her humble way to comfort Mrs. Kirkpatrick and others in similar conditions.

Because Mabel was singing happily, she realized that God was changing her heart. While working for Mrs. Snodgrass, she had hoped to never again work in a hotel; and now she was happily doing it. She was also thankful that she had learned how to do her work thoroughly. Yes, God knew she would someday need that training which she got while working for Mrs. McNally and Mrs. Snodgrass. Now Mabel understood the verse, *All things work together for good to them that love God, to them who are the called according to his purpose.*

Homeless people also migrated to Corpus Christi because they could better survive the winter. Walking to work and back home again, Mabel passed rows and rows of small houses where barefoot, ragged children played in the streets. Out of her meager wages, she sometimes bought candy or other treats for the children. Often she stopped and talked with sad-looking women. Some women told her their troubles. Mabel would tell them how God had helped her, and she encouraged them to also trust in Him. Her compassion caused others to be happier. Neither did Mabel ignore the beggars. She shared what she had with those who were crippled, blind, or old and feeble.

One neighbor noticed this and asked, "Why do you share with the beggars?"

"I believe God wants me to help the poor," Mabel answered. "For the Bible says, *He that hath mercy on the poor, happy is he.* It also says, *Blessed is he that considers the poor; the Lord will deliver him in time of trouble.*"

Mabel pitied the sick and poor wherever she saw them, but she pitied her sick Papa more than she pitied anyone else. She bought fresh fruit for him whenever she could. She cooked his meals, she massaged his arms, legs, and back, and did everything she could to help him feel more comfortable.

For weeks now, Papa had not been able to lie down. He sat day and night in a chair. To sleep, he placed his arms over the back of another chair and laid his head on his arms.

Before going to work, Mabel prepared his breakfast and placed it on the table beside his chair. She couldn't wait until he had finished eating, because he had to rest between every few bites, thus taking a long—long—time to eat. Each day she wondered how she would find him when she returned home.

One morning, after he had struggled to breathe through the night, Mabel asked, "Do you think this warm climate is helping you?"

"I don't know," he said slowly, as if almost too weak to talk. "I do know—my health is failing fast. I have been—wanting to talk to you—and see what you think. You suppose—we had better go back to Oklahoma City?" He rested awhile then continued. "There we have a lot of good friends and the people at the Church. It might be better for you to be near them."

Mabel felt dizzy. She held the bed post to steady herself. She knew Papa might be near death. What would she do if he died? Mabel thought, *Oh, if Albert would come right now, like he did that night so long ago in Mangum when I felt so alone. That was years ago. But surely Albert is still hunting for us, like I'm hunting for him.*

"Mabel, why don't you talk? Don't you want to go back to Oklahoma City?" Papa was saying.

"Oh, yes, Papa, it might be better. We have no family here. We had better be near old friends and church people as to be among strangers." Mabel remembered reading in Mrs. Lou's diary that her baby had died while they were among strangers.

Two weeks later Mabel and Papa left beautiful Corpus Christi. "I hope I can come and live here again," Mabel said, as she watched the city disappear behind them.

There was money from Mabel's savings to rent a small apartment in Oklahoma City and buy a few groceries. As soon as she got Papa settled, she went to look for a job. She could not wait to find one that paid well, or one she enjoyed. She would take any available job. God blessed her to get a job again in the Wilson Meat Packing House where she had worked when they moved to Oklahoma City after leaving Webb City.

The following Sunday, Mabel went to the little Church of God chapel on Eighth Street where they had attended before. Mrs. Lou Hightower, Alvin, Jim, and Aubrey were there; also, Mrs. Hunter, and Ira Stover with his wife, Ruby. How great to see familiar people, hear old hymns and inspired sermons. Mabel was especially glad to see Alvin.

Questions for reflection:

1. What lesson about money did Mabel learn while living in Corpus Christi?
2. Why was Mabel confident she would be with her family again?
3. In what ways had Mabel changed?
4. What Bible verse did Mabel now understand?
5. How did Mabel treat others?

...I will never leave thee, nor forsake thee.

Hebrew 13:5

THOSE DARK DAYS

Mabel awoke to the sounds of the Oklahoma wind. It seemed almost like a dream that they were again living in Oklahoma City. Papa's health had not improved while in Webb City, Missouri. Neither had their stay in sunny Corpus Christi, Texas helped him. He had steadily grown weaker and weaker, so they came back to Oklahoma City. Now they were near the church people whom Papa believed would assist Mabel if he became helpless. Attending church with old friends and finding a job at the Wilson Meat Packing where the Hightowers, Alvin, Cornelius, Jim, and their uncle, Mr. Sharp, were working, made Mabel feel at home.

One morning when Mabel came to work, she saw Alvin standing inside the door of the elevator he operated. His hands, face, and clothes were wet and spotted with blood. "What's happened?" she gasped!

"Just look at this mess," he said, pointing to himself and the elevator. Mabel peeked inside the elevator. Blood and small pieces of meat were splattered on the walls; animal bones lay on the floor. She covered her mouth and nose to keep out the stench of fresh blood.

"I think the elevator cable must have broken. We fell all the way from the third floor! It's a miracle that this container of garbage didn't dump over and run down into the shaft," Alvin said.

"Haven't you had trouble before with this elevator?" Mabel asked.

"Yes, I have. A few months ago it crashed into the ceiling. At the speed we were going, it's a wonder we didn't break an opening in the roof and go sailing out into space."

"Now that would have been funny, only you might have been killed, and that would have been terrible," Mabel said. They both laughed. "I'm so sorry," she added "but I must hurry on or I will be late."

Mabel felt sorry that Alvin was having trouble. Nevertheless, just seeing him had made her day. She loved the sound of his soft voice. She hurriedly put on her cap and big rubber apron. The cap kept the meat clean of hairs, and the apron was supposed to keep her clothes clean, although often it did not.

Although Mabel had to leave Papa alone during the day while she went out to work, she trusted God to care for him. God had promised her long ago that, *"He would never leave nor forsake her,"* and He never had. Each morning when Mabel kissed Papa goodbye, she would whisper to him, *"I will never leave thee, nor forsake thee."* She also hoped he wouldn't fall and lie on the floor until she returned. He couldn't possible get up by himself, now that his body was so full of water.

His legs were now almost as big as his waist had been. His arms were as big as his legs used to be. All this fullness of water made it almost impossible to walk, and, of course, more difficult to breath. He could not lie down. He sat in a chair with both arms placed over the back of another chair directly in front of him. For sleeping, Mabel placed a pillow over the chair back, and Papa would lay his big bushy head on the pillow and sleep a little at a time.

Some days when he felt very weak, Mabel stayed home with him. However, missing a day at work meant losing a day's wages, and losing a day's wages meant doing without something they needed.

Papa became so full of water that his skin cracked and the water started dripping out. These breaks soon turned into draining sores. Mabel got up very early and carefully bandaged these sores. Then she prepared their meals before going to work. After working nine hours, she prepared supper; then she cleaned and bandaged his sores again. Often through the night, she got out of bed and helped him.

Days, weeks, and months passed as Mabel worked during the day at Wilson's and nursed Papa at night. Mabel often prayed that Albert would come to see Papa before he died. She also wanted her brother near at a time like this.

One day when Mabel came home, Papa said, "The doctor came today."

"What did he say?" Mabel asked.

He said, "Living in Oklahoma is killing you, Mr. Kelley. In winter, the dry cold air is making breathing difficult. In the summer, dust particles in the air are clogging up your air passages. If you expect to get well, you should move south, somewhere near a lake or the gulf, so you can be outside in the sun and breathe fresh clean air year round."

"Oh, Papa, you think it would help?"

"I told him, see that trunk over there? Mabel has packed our belongings in it many times, and we have moved here and there for years. Every time we moved, I hoped to get well; yet, I am steadily getting weaker. I think Mabel has moved her last time with me. The next move I make will be straight up to Heaven. And I'll have to make that trip alone."

"Oh, Papa, don't say that. You can't leave me. What would I do without you?"

"I'm—sorry," he said slowly. "I—hate to leave you. I know you will miss me. But Mabel, I'm a lot of trouble. I make so much work for you. Remember, Jesus said, *'I will never leave thee nor forsake thee.'* God will be with you when I am gone."

Mabel smiled, "Why Papa, that's the verse I tell you every day; and Papa, I love nursing you. I love you, Papa. Don't leave me." Mabel remembered that day so long ago when Officer Martin found Papa. That day Papa had said. "I won't leave you. You will leave me when you get married." That was twelve years ago, and the one Mabel hoped to marry still had not showed her any special attention. Although they were good friends, and he often came and helped with Papa. Mabel brushed Papa's bushy hair back from his forehead and kissed it. "Papa, I love you," she whispered.

The people from the Church of God found out about Papa's weakened condition and started checking on him while Mabel was at work. Soon they had coordinated teams to sit with him. Someone would sit a while in the day and others a while at night.

Mabel had read in the Bible where Jesus said, *I was sick and ye visited me; and his disciples asked, When saw we thee sick and visited thee? And he answered them, Inasmuch as you have done it unto one of the least of these my brethren, ye have done it unto me.* Mabel realized the people were helping Papa as if he were Jesus!

Many different men and women from the church came to stay at night with Papa; however, Alvin and Mrs. Lou came most often. Alvin stayed many nights with Papa so Mabel could rest; then he would work the following day just as Mabel did. Mabel appreciated Alvin's help. What would she do without it?

"Mabel, you must go to bed," Alvin insisted on that night in October. "You need strength for the days ahead. I will sit beside your papa. I promise to take good care of him."

"I hate to leave him. He seems so weak." She said. Then she kissed Papa and whispered, *"I will never leave thee nor forsake thee."*

When Mabel awoke the following morning, Papa was lying down on the bed. She knew he had slipped away quietly during the night, because he could not lie down and breathe. "My papa, my papa," she cried, kneeling beside him. "I will miss you, but I know you need this rest."

Mrs. Lou and Alvin stayed that day with Mabel. They called the undertaker and helped her arrange for Papa's funeral.

Questions for reflection:

1. What did Mabel whisper to Papa when she left each morning?
2. What did Mabel do at night while others were sleeping?
3. What did the church do to help Mabel?
4. What commandment was the church practicing?
5. Who came most often to help Mabel?
6. What were Mabel's last words to Papa?

Not one family member was there to share Mabel's loss, to cry with her,
to share sweet memories, to plan for the future, to support one another
in life without Papa. No brother, nor sister, no aunt, nor uncle, cousin
nor grandparent were beside her to help pay the funeral expenses,
nor to help her select a stone to mark where dear Papa was buried.

If ye love me keep my commandments. And I will pray the Father, and he shall give you another Comforter, that he may abide with you forever;

John 14:15-16

A GREAT CHANGE

The dreaded day had come, and Albert wasn't there. Mabel stood in the cemetery beside Papa lying in his casket. Papa's last words rang in her ears. *"You have been a wonderful—loving daughter to me. No other child—could have been better—I hate to leave—to leave you——to face life's problems alone—yet I have no other choice—I'm sorry to have caused you so much trouble."*

"Oh, Papa, my Papa," Mabel had cried, *"I'd be glad to care for you if you could stay. I—I—I—don't want you to leave me. Neither do I want you to suffer,"* she had added.

For many months, Mabel had had mixed feelings. A battle raged inside her. She didn't want Papa to suffer, but she didn't want him to die either.

Finally, he had gone on to his rest. Now he wasn't suffering any more, but Mabel felt so alone, so strange and fearful! Not one family member was there to share her loss, to cry with her, to share sweet memories, to plan for the future, to support one another in life without Papa. No brother, nor sister, no aunt, nor uncle, cousin nor grandparent were beside her to help pay the funeral expenses, nor to help her select a stone to mark where dear Papa was buried.

Then, like heavenly music, she heard the church people singing, *Feet that have carried the gospel glad, tidings of peace as the Savior has said, Hands that have strengthened the weak and sad, will be waiting there.* Mabel remembered how Papa had walked for miles to comfort and pray for the sick, how his big strong hands had helped the widows and the poor in the years when he was strong. Yes, Papa would be waiting for her. Then they sang, *Waiting and beckoning on, and on, resting from toil in that palace home, eager to know, will the children come to these mansions fair?*

Yes, Papa, you rest and I will be coming, Mabel said in her heart. I *will always love and serve Jesus. He is my best friend. Yes, Papa, I will come to see you.*

The music of the songs died away and all was silent except for wind rustling the brown leaves on the trees. Then the minister read John 14. *Let not your heart be troubled...In my father's house are many mansions...I go to prepare a place for you...I will come again, and receive you unto myself; that where I am there ye may be also...I will pray the Father and he shall give you another Comforter, that he may abide with you forever...I will not leave you comfortless...*

Mabel heard a man's voice say, "Amen." She looked to the side and saw that Alvin had stepped up beside her. For just a moment, the heaviness left. She wanted to fall into his arms and feel his protective embrace around her. She wanted to cry forever on his shoulder, although it would have been inappropriate for a single Christian woman who barely allowed her ankles to show below her skirt. Besides, deep in her heart, Mabel knew God would be near and comfort her. She wouldn't give in to her emotions.

After the preaching and the singing were over, the saints gathered around Mabel. They said comforting words, but Mabel hardly heard them. She felt desolate, like she would rather die than return to the awful, silent loneliness of the apartment. She looked at the casket, wishing that the lid would pop open and Papa would smile again at her. The big hole under the casket was dark. She didn't want Papa to be put down into the ground. How could she let her loving Papa, the one she had nursed and kept comfortable for so long, be put in a hole and covered with cold dirt?

She wanted to run, to run away from it all---to run and run and run to a place that had no more sickness and death. Even so, she couldn't move. Her feet seemed glued to the earth beside Papa's casket. She could not make them leave. She could not take a step.

Mabel felt a hand on her shoulder. Looking around, she saw Mrs. Lou and Alvin. He was smiling at her, but his eyes were red and swollen. She knew he had been sharing her grief, for he had been crying. "Alvin and I will go with you to the apartment and get your things. You must come home and stay a while with us." Hope filled her heart, and rushing back into her memory came her favorite childhood verse, *Weeping may endure for a night but joy cometh in the morning.* Alvin put out his arm offering his support. Mabel took hold of it as she moved away from her beloved Papa. She was taking her first step into a different season of her life.

That night when Mabel was lying in bed and all was quiet, she thought about the many times that Alvin and Mrs. Lou had helped her. In her most difficult days, it seemed that they always appeared. When she was weary and couldn't do her work, they came to do it or sent someone else to do it. When she needed sleep, they stayed up with Papa and let her rest. *I thank You, Jesus, for these friends who have taken the place of the family I do not have. Thank You for rewarding me for the times I helped others. You have kept your promise that says, if we give you will give back to us more than we have given. Jesus, Your Word is a great source of comfort, and You have also put people in my life to comfort me.*

Mabel then opened her Bible to the 21st chapter of Revelations and read. *God shall wipe away all tears from their eyes; and there shall be no more death, neither sorrow, nor crying, neither shall there be any more pain;... I make all things new... Thank You God for this promise. Yes, someday all things will be new. I thank You that Papa is now in the land where everything is forever new. And, God, I believe that I will soon begin a new life. Good night, Jesus, my Friend.*

Mabel's heart was happy while staying with the Hightower family. It felt glorious to be in a family where humans were talking, laughing or fussing. Yes, even fussing sounded good to Mabel after such a long time of hearing the laborious breathing of Papa. Being around Mrs. Lou again was also like being young and full of hope and faith, like when she first met Mrs. Lou. Mabel recalled that first year in Oklahoma City, and how she had kept up her courage by repeating to herself the verse, *I can do all things through Christ who strengthens me,* Philippians 4:13. She praised God that she had found Papa and was able to nurse him through his years of sickness. What mixed emotions, a heart full of gratitude and a heart full of sorrow at the same time.

Also there was something about being around Alvin that caused her to feel secure. It was similar to the feeling of being with Papa. Secretly she had wished for years that Alvin would notice her as more than just a friend. During Papa's last weeks, though, Alvin had sat up many nights with Papa and let Mabel rest, proving that he was more than an ordinary friend.

Mabel gathered courage after a few days at the Hightower's home. She knew she couldn't stay with them forever. She had to go on living without them and without Papa. She must face the loneliness—and conquer it. *I can do all things through Christ who strengthens me,* Mabel told herself for the hundredth time. *Yes, I can. I can go on. I will choose to be thankful when grief strikes, when it coils itself around me and would strangle me; I will thank God for my present blessings. There are always many things for which to be thankful.*

Back in her apartment, Mabel took Papa's two best shirts and folded them carefully. These, and the lamp that sat beside his bed, his pictures, a couple of poems he had written, the letters he had sent while they were separated, and a few other things—these she placed carefully into her trunk. *This is all I have left of my dear Papa,* she said.

From the first day Mabel went back to live in her apartment, Alvin came everyday to see about her. He never stayed at her apartment more than a few minutes; yet it comforted Mabel to know someone was watching over her!

One evening about two weeks after Papa died, Mabel heard a gentle tapping on her door. When she opened it, Alvin was there. She noticed he was unusually nervous. He stood holding his hat with both hands right over his heart. He shifted his weight from one foot to another as he asked a simple question, "Just wondered if you would like to go for a ride this evening?"

"I'd love too," Mabel answered. She slipped on her sweater and followed him to his car in the street. His Reo car was high off the ground. Alvin opened the car door and Mabel climbed in.

He cranked up the motor, and they bounced over the rough brick streets of what is known as Brick Town in Oklahoma City. They shouted above the roar of the motor about things they saw along the way. The vibrations of the rough streets shook Mabel's hair pins loose. She kept busy replacing them as they fell.

Mabel had met Alvin twelve years ago when she was doing housework for his mother. Twelve years ago, Mabel was not thinking of getting married. She was only seventeen, and her main interest was in finding her papa. Nevertheless, she did appreciate Alvin for his noble character and hoped secretly he would also notice her Christian character. Their paths had crossed many times in those twelve years. They worked at Wilson Meat Packing house at the same time. Often at church service they saw each other. Also, Alvin had moved with his family to Arkansas, and Mabel had moved several times with her Papa to others cities and states.

Alvin had noticed Mabel was honest, humble, and a good worker. Many of the girls whom his mother hired were careless, dishonest, or proud. Later, when he visited the church where she attended, he was impressed with her song leading ability, for he also loved to sing. These last few years they attended the same church and both worked at Wilson's Meat Packing House and had developed a great friendship, but they had never gone out for a special evening alone.

As they were driving around, Alvin cleared his throat and coughed a little; then said, "I want to ask you something." He said no more. Then they talked about other things for a while, and again he cleared his throat and said, "I want to ask you something." A little later in the evening he again said, "I want to ask you something."

Mabel thought she knew what he wanted to ask, so after him saying, "I want to ask you something," several more times, she said, "Alvin, what is it you want to ask me?"

He coughed and cleared his throat, then was silent for a long time as if he couldn't speak. He just kept clearing his throat, but no words came out.

By now, Mabel was really feeling sorry for poor Alvin. She felt sure she knew what he wanted to asked, so she said, "Alvin, do you want to ask if I would marry you?"

"Yes, yes, that—that is what I wanted to say. How did you know?"

Mabel just shrugged her shoulders and put another hairpin back into her braid. Before the evening was over, Alvin and Mabel planned their wedding.

That night before going to bed, Mabel prayed: *Thank You, God, for turning my weeping into joy, for watching over me and giving me someone with whom to share my life. Thank You for filling my lonely heart with happiness. God, I will work hard to make a happy, godly home. Help me to be content always with whatever Alvin provides. And please, oh, please, Lord, if you give me any children, let me live until they are grown. Lord,*

I don't want my children to be without a mother as I have been. I praise You, God for this happy day.

Mabel May Kelley and Alvin Robert Hightower were married in the Church of God on November 3, 1929.

Questions for reflection:

1. Who was with Mabel when Papa died?
2. Why did Mabel feel so lonely at Papa's funeral?
3. Why does Mabel believe she will see her family again?
4. Who took Mabel home after the funeral?
5. Did God keep his promise to comfort Mabel?
6. What kind of attitude does Mabel show in her prayers?

Mabel May Kelley and Alvin Robert Hightower were married in Oklahoma City, OK at the Church of God on November 3, 1929

The End

A LITTLE ABOUT MABEL'S FAMILY

Mabel loved family and longed to have a future one of her own. She spoke often of her beloved Papa's family living in McDonald County, Missouri, where she lived her first seven years. I remember her speaking of her uncles, Henry, William, and John, two aunts (one named Tomlinson Grissom), and her cousins John, Doyal, and Lorn.

Simon Pleasant Andrew Kelly, Mabel's father, was born in April of 1861 in Kentucky. His father, also named Simon Kelley, and mother (surnamed Griscall) were from Tennessee. Simon Kelley's ancestors came from Ireland. According to him, their original name was O'Kelley. The large Kelley family settled in Greene County, Tennessee. The area later became known as "Kelley Gap." They migrated to Kentucky, where Simon Pleasant Andrew was born and later into McDonald County, Missouri where Mabel was born.

The Pineville and Neosho, Missouri genealogy departments of the public library have information about the Kelley family for anyone interested in researching. There are some interesting stories.

Simon Pleasant Andrew Kelley married a woman from England, and they claimed land in Oklahoma during one of the "Oklahoma Land Runs." While in Oklahoma, a son and daughter were born: Albert Henry on September 6, 1893 and Estella M. on October 4, 1895. His wife died in Oklahoma. (Albert was last seen in Mangum, Oklahoma, about 1912.) On May 10, 1917, Estella married James Wallace Adair. She gave birth to two children, a son, Harred or Harold on October 12, 1918 and a daughter, Geraldine, on July 12, 1919. Estella was buried in Granite, OK in 1925.

The 1900 United States Census records show Simon Pleasant Andrew Kelley living back in Pineville and married to Mary E. Williams. This new wife, Mary, was born in April, 1877 in Missouri. Mary's father, Myres

(Mike) H. Williams was born in North Carolina. Her mother, Isabelle was born in Ohio. Mary was of Dutch ancestry. Mabel was born to Simon and Mary on October 1 of that year, 1900. A younger son, John, was born in 1905. He died four years later in 1909. Mary died in 1907 and is buried in Elliot Cemetery southwest of Neosho, Missouri.

Mabel loved her family and kept searching for her brother, Albert, until she was unable to do so.

Mabel May Kelley married Alvin Robert Hightower on November 3, 1929. To this union a son, James Pleasant, was born on September 17, 1930. Also, they had three daughters Lois May (Hightower) Davis, May 23, 1932; Roberta Lee (Hightower) Gaines, April 25, 1933; and Charlotte Nell (Hightower) Huskey, August 25, 1935. In 1938, Mabel gave birth to triplet sons, that did not survive.

Mabel's husband and her four children. I like to imagine
that Mabel is watching over her family, sending angels
to their rescue whenever any need help.

This is all of Mabel's children and grandchildren except
one daughter, Lois, and a grandson, Donald Alvin.

Mabel prayed that she would live until her children were adults. When she died on September 21, 1964, her youngest child, Charlotte Huskey, was 29 years old.

This is Charlotte Huskey and her family a year after Mabel's death.

Mabel's grand daughter, Patricia (Huskey) Bell with her
husband, James Bell and 11 of their 15 grand children. This
is only a part of Mabel's 32 great, great grandchildren.

Mabel has four children, 12 grandchildren, 51 great-grandchildren,
and 32 great-great-grandchildren, with more coming. All these together,
with their spouses, make a wonderful family. I like to imagine that Mabel
is watching over her big family, sending angels to their rescue whenever
anyone needs help.

Read *Our Father in Heaven* sub-titled *Mabel's Family* and learn about
her four children.

Acknowledgements

This book was successfully completed because of the encouragement of people who felt that the story of Mabel's life could also bless others. The first to probe me was Marie (Pruitt) Miles, board member of the Faith Publishing House and an author herself. To accompany the Bible lessons she was writing, she needed examples of people living out the *Fruits of the Spirit*. It was easy to find examples of the fruits of the spirit, (*love, joy, peace, long suffering, gentleness, faith, meekness and temperance*) in my mother's daily life. The lessons were for children, so I wrote the stories that mother had told me about her childhood. These stories were first published in the Beautiful Way Sunday school periodical of the Church of God. From that time, I have received many requests for more stories about Mabel. This book includes her life story until she married.

Those who kept me motivated were my wonderful children, their faithful spouses, and my delightful grandchildren. Because of their consistent encouragement this book has been written.

I wish to thank those who read and reread my manuscripts and corrected many errors: Tricia Bell, Roberta Gaines, Karen Goltry, Sandra Melot, Irma Sallee, Clifford Smith and Nelda Sorrell.

Last but not least, I thank my husband, James, who has for many years sacrificed "our time together" to allow me to write.

Dedicated to my family,
Who has assisted in writing this book.
You placed hope in my heart
And dreams in my head.
You've been a shoulder to lean on
And an ear to listen.

You're my biggest cheerleaders
And my kindest critics.
You think about me way too much,
But I am glad you do;
Because you are not just my family,
You are my best friends, too!

About the author

Charlotte and her siblings lived on a farm in Oregon with "Mabel," the best of mothers. She married missionary dentist, James Huskey. They did evangelistic and humanitarian work in Mexico for 23 years.

For 15 years Charlotte wrote children's weekly Bible Lessons and illustrative stories for the Church of God Sunday School magazine. She has published several book-length serial stories, including, *The What Would Jesus Do Club* and *The Nutty Nutritional Club*, also, biographies of Ahn Ei Shook, Lillian Trasher (The Nile Mother), and Jaya Kollipara. Charlotte is a lifelong student of 'family life,' continually researching and writing about family issues.

Much of her published works have been translated into other languages.

Printed in the United States
By Bookmasters